LIONS
to
LAMBS

**FINDING PEACE
IN THE MIDST OF HARDSHIPS**

CASSIA TAYLOR

Copyright © 2015 by Cassia Taylor
eBook and paper edition available at Amazon.com
Discover more about the author and purchase paper back at
www.cassiataylor.org

All rights reserved. No portion of this book may be reproduced, stored in a retrieval system, or transmitted in any form or by any means-electronic, mechanical, photocopy, recording, scanning, or other-except for brief quotations in critical reviews or articles, without the prior written permission of the author.
Scripture quotations are from the King James Version of the Bible. Public domain.

Edited by: Susan Wilson
Cover Photo: Emily Soto
Cover Design: Michelle Taormina

Special Thanks to my husband for all of his support and encouragement. My family for loving me through all of my mistakes and hardships. To my amazing editors: Susan Wilson and Barbara Hamilton. Most of all Jesus. For without the guidance of the Holy Spirit, this book would not be here.

Table of Contents

Introduction..i

1. A Fighter is Born 1
2. My Father's Story 7
3. Discovering My Template 19
4. Correcting My Template 25
5. Correcting With Love 29
6. Misplaced Convictions 35
7. Drawing My Sword 45
8. Timing Is Everything 63
9. Letting Go Of Natural Abilities 69
10. Becoming Weak To Help The Weak 77
11. The Lamb Has Emerged 83
12. Be Faithful In The Little Things 91
13. God's Timing, Not Ours 95
14. Hold Tightly Onto God's Promises 101
15. God's Promises Followed By Trials 109
16. Facing Our Weaknesses 117
17. Finally Baptized 123
18. God's Unconditional Love 131
19. Fear And Faith Contradict 141
20. Victory In The Work Place 149
21. A Lesson In Humility 157
22. Victim or Victor- A Real Life Bible Story 167
23. The Hardest Trial Of All 179

Epilogue 187

INTRODUCTION

I never thought I could write a book. When I think back to my school days, I do not remember ever being taught how to properly write or spell. Somehow, I slipped through the public school system without anyone noticing. When it came time for me to write the following words, I had to completely trust God for His help. There is a bumper sticker that reads, "If you can read this, thank a teacher." Well, if you are reading this, thank God. I consider it a small miracle.

My life has been a journey across high mountains and through deep valleys, figuratively speaking. The fact that I am in a place now where I feel secure in God and in life and can experience peace and joy is yet another miracle. I want to share what I have learned along the way. I believe in that old cliché that things happen for a reason. That reason, in part, is to be able to relay the truths God has taught me and to share how I learned to handle some of the difficult experiences I had to face.

Throughout my life, I lacked the inner peace that I desperately wanted. Anxious and in turmoil, I found it difficult to respond correctly to the many challenges presented to me. My faith was not strong enough to believe that God would help me arrive on the upside of my situation. I did not trust fully that He was in control of my circumstances and that made it more difficult to listen to the wisdom set forth in His word, the Bible. Because of my disobedience, I found myself in constant conflict with those around me. I was unable to reap God's blessings or to have many Christ-like components in my life.

The characteristics I am referring to as Christ-like attributes are also given the term, "fruit," in the Bible. They are characteristic traits such as love, self-control, joy, peace, kindness, goodness, faithfulness, meekness, and virtue. After many years of facing one difficult situation after another, I have finally learned how maintain a sense of peace in the midst of the challenges of life. My life finally demonstrates these so-called fruits. Although I have not enjoyed all the difficult experiences, the very circumstances I disliked are exactly what enabled me to become the optimistic, healthy, joyous person I am today.

It will be my goal in the following pages to demonstrate how to look at and convert difficult circumstances into personal and spiritual growth. It is only through the grace and mercy of God that we can begin to see that He has a purpose for the obstacles we face during our lifetime. As God tells us, **"Every Scripture is God-breathed (given by His inspiration) and profitable for instruction, for reproof and conviction of sin, for correction of error and discipline in obedience, [and] for training in righteousness in holy living, in conformity to God's will in thought, purpose, and action so that the man of God may be complete and proficient, well fitted and thoroughly equipped for every good work.** (II Timothy 3:16-17)

My words do not come to you as a seasoned, ordained pastor or a divinity scholar; they come merely from me, a young woman, who has experienced a series of challenging
events in life that have taught me some valuable lessons and truths. My sincere hope is to share some thoughts on

how to avoid wasting time and energy and how to best respond to life's inevitable hardships while incorporating a stronger belief in our God and Savior.

In this book, I will walk you through some of the trials that have occurred in my life. I want you to ask yourself as you are reading, "Would I have made the same choices?" I hope this book does not end up collecting dust on a shelf. Instead, I would like it to become a reference book and a tool to remind and enable you to look at the moments that stand out in your life and to ask God to reveal the purpose of these pivotal events. They really do have a purpose whether you have placed your life into God's hands, or not.

I feel it is important to note that never once did I think of myself as a victim. I never felt it was beneficial to maintain that mindset. Many people feel victimized by life. It is important to mention, I think, that some of our difficulties are self-imposed because of our own poor choices. Other difficult circumstances occur separately from the consequences of our individual choices and are the result of someone else's choices. Other times, our difficulties are just part of life. Regardless of the source, the important thing is to avoid feeling like a victim in life. If you are already experiencing this unfortunate belief, I want to help you by showing you how to break free from this mentality by immersing yourself in the wisdom of God and relying upon the love of Jesus.

Along with the painful feeling that life has somehow been stacked against us, fear and insecurity can be present as we face challenging situations. When we recognize how much God loves us though, we can gain enough faith and hope to overcome all the negativity. It is impossible to succumb to negative feelings and beliefs when we truly know how deeply God loves us. As stated in

1 John 4:18, **"Perfect love casts out all fear."** Knowing and receiving God's love eliminates the need, for example, to worry what others might think of us. God already accepts and loves us in this very moment. There is no action required to conjure up the care and love that He has for us. It is a gift and, therefore, a given. We do not have to busy ourselves with every Christian conference, every church service, every home group, or every opportunity to volunteer to meet everyone's needs. You know what I mean. Think of a parent's love. It is to be hoped that you had a positive experience as a child and knew that, without a doubt, when push came to shove, your parent would be there for you. Well, God is even better at that. In fact, He is perfect and He loves you with pure, unconditional love.

Somehow, we get excessively focused on our adversities. Try to think of adversity as something God is using to help us improve as human beings. If we just trust Him and refrain from complaining, He will get us through the challenges, and we will experience peace during life's frequent tests. God desires to fill each one of us with faith, hope, and love and all the positive outcomes once those are in place. Without fear, we can be bold and courageous. With hope, we can be patient and stand firm. With love, we can feel strong and secure. With peace, we can actually enjoy the process. God is good.

I never had anyone to help guide me through my hardships; I did not have access to anyone whose real life experiences related to my life. I felt very alone in my struggles and confused. It was only through my mistakes, constant trial and error, and through my relationship with the God, ad stories from the bible, that I was able to hear and receive His corrections and gain the direction and instruction I needed.

I have stated that God's love is unconditional. There is a catch, but it is not too bad and only for our benefit. In order to receive all that God has in store for us, we need to acknowledge that we are not perfect. We need to admit that some of our thoughts and actions are just plain icky. The way we are living our lives does not line up with the truth of who God wants us to be as stated in the Word of God. Our goal then should be to try to allow the Holy Spirit to help us rid our lives of the things we do that oppose that truth. Our own efforts will never result in becoming the perfect person. It is impossible, but Jesus fills that gap for us and He will lead us across the bridge into heaven when the time comes. In the meantime, we need to be patient with ourselves, just as God is patient with us as we allow Him to transform us.

My hope is that in writing this, I can also help bridge a gap, and can help those of you who struggle in life to not have to struggle quite as much as I did. I definitely learned the hard way and I believe I have learned some things along the way. It is to be hoped that I can provide you with a schedule for the direct train through the proverbial wilderness to the promised land and help you to avoid taking 40 years to complete a journey that geographically should have taken the Israelites a mere 11 days. I hope that you will be able to use my trials, tribulations, and all I have learned as tools to create a shortcut through your mess and to arrive at a positive outcome in your circumstances (aided by the guidance of God's Holy Spirit).

Chapter 1
A Fighter Is Born

It was 1979. In the distance were the alarming sounds of a fire truck and an ambulance. As the emergency vehicles got closer to their destination, the wail of the sirens got louder. Lying in the arms of a desperate mother was an infant child, slowly slipping away. The mother watched in fear as the infant's face turned from ashen grey to blue to deep purple. She knew that her precious child would not make it another minute. In desperation, she cried out, "Jesus! Jesus!" Instantly the child's airways opened and she began to cry.

My mother told me of this miracle long before I could comprehend its meaning. I was, of course, too small to remember the impact that it had on me; however, I feel that my spirit never forgot. Something was planted deep within me the day the Lord saved my life. I became a fighter and a survivor against all odds.

I love the scripture in the Bible, John 16:33 that states, **"I have said these things to you, that in me you may have peace. In the world you will have tribulation. But take heart; I have overcome the world."** This scripture has always filled me with faith and hope particularly because of the word, "peace". People do not focus enough on that word in this scripture. God is telling us exactly how to get through the difficult events that happen in our lives. Life's trials are inevitable for us all. James 1:2-4 states, **"Consider it pure joy, my brothers, whenever you face trials of many kings, because you know that the testing of your faith develops perseverance. Perseverance must finish its work so that you may be mature and complete, not lacking anything."** We can experience hope if we focus on the blessing that will come out of the trials instead of focusing on the trial itself. God offers us the inner peace we need to help us get through the difficult aspects of life. He does not expect us to deal with anything alone. It is just a matter, then, of learning how to receive the sense of peace that He has to offer.

Instead of directing our focus toward acquiring peace, our tendency is to focus on the hardships of the trial. We allow the pain that comes with hard times to distract us instead of help us. Peace is readily available to all who believe in Jesus and we need to figure out how to grab hold of it and not let it go.

Year after year, trial after trial, I failed to learn how to maintain that inner peace. Finally, I learned the valuable secret to look at my challenging circumstances in a different light. It is fine to feel the pain; in fact, it is impossible not to. At some point, however, we need to allow God to help us overcome our pain so we can look at our trials through His eyes. We need to understand that difficulties exist to change things in us that fall short of who God wants us to be. This is not to add pressure on anyone. It is simply a reminder that God wants so much more for us than we are currently experiencing.

The purpose of our trials is to bring us to a higher capacity of awareness of Christ characteristics. To allow us an opportunity for a righteous, healthy, and joyous spiritual growth. To increase our vision of who we are in Christ. How do we do this? God's word teaches us how to walk in obedience with His principles. It is important to note that God does not need us to be better for His sake, but for our own. Through applications of the principles of scriptures, we are able to reap the benefits and enjoy righteousness, peace, joy, love, all of God's blessings. God really does care about us. He wants us to have a good life. Scriptures can only prove their power in our lives if we live them out and apply them to our situations.

We are all born with distinct personality characteristics. They are what make us unique. For example, I am courageous, bold, confident, and fearless. I was born with all the attributes of a lion. My family and friends have always called me a lion, confirming what I know to be true. I have always had faith that I could do anything. I will tell you this story as an example: When I was two years old, my aunt lost her purse. Everyone in the house was frantically looking for it. My mother said, "Cassia, you need to help us find the lost purse." Rather than joining the others in their frenzy, I said with faith and confidence, "I prayed." Knowing God would help them find it, I believed there was no need to look. Immediately, after I prayed, my aunt found her purse. My family members still talk about that incident of 34 years ago. They wonder how a little girl could have that much faith. I guess that is what the scripture means when it refers to unquestioning faith as having "faith like a child". I will admit that as I got older, my faith was tested along with many other virtues, and I did not and still do not always pass the test.

I grew up in a very poor household. My father worked pouring concrete ten or more hours a day in the Florida heat. He worked hard, but there still never seemed to be much money. I disliked being poor, but always hung on to the scripture in Romans 8:28 as a way to get through, **"And we know that in all things God works for the good of those who love him, who have been called according to his purpose."** This scripture filled me with hope that I would not live in poverty forever and, more specifically, hope that I would have food to eat at night. However, it is not until now that I am able to look back at my life and see all of the benefit I received from the way I grew up and from the dependence I had upon the words of this scripture. At that time, it was all about God supplying my physical needs of food, clothing, and shelter. Oftentimes we read these encouraging scriptures and interpret them in terms of financial blessing. However, God had other kinds of blessings in store. That is why we must continue to trust in God and know that He knows best what we need most. Blessings come in various and sundry forms. Not only do blessings come in different forms, but also at different times throughout our lives. God truly turned a bad living environment into a training ground to help cultivate my Christ-like characteristics. To me, that is more precious than gold.

After thirty-five years of trials, I realize that the best outcome of these situations are the peace, joy, hope, faith, and love that God has added to my life as a result. God promises to give us "peace that passes all understanding." That kind of peace removes the deep pain and confusion of life's difficult times and enables us to replace the negative emotions with actual and deeply felt positive experiences. This is what God wants for us and He will put us through what ever we can handle in order to get us to the place where we experience these blessings. If we can have peace during our trials, we will be able to see so much more clearly what the purpose of that trial is. Peace comes when we trust that God is with us. **"Be strong and courageous. Do not be afraid or terrified because of them, for the Lord our God goes with you; he will never leave you nor forsake you."** (Deuteronomy 31:6). It is imperative to trust that God is with us. When we trust Him, we will have the understanding that trials are not punishment, but rather, tools. They are a means to an end; training for a more fulfilling life. Never believe that God has turned His back just because life gets difficult. As you read on, you will learn about many of the poor choices that I made during my trials simply because I lacked the understanding of this principle. You will also learn how I was able to stop fighting against God and start fighting for Him.

Chapter 2

My Father's Story

Poverty is such a misunderstood word. I know that there are many extremes and definitions of poverty and that poverty in the United States differs in meaning from poverty in other third world countries. When I describe my childhood, it is in context of the United States and it was then, as a child, that I lived in poverty.

I was born in Tennessee. When I was three years old my family moved to central Florida. We moved from a tiny little trailer into a three bedroom, two bathroom house. To me, it was a mansion.

My father, as I said, was a hardworking man. He was also an abusive man. He had fits of anger, was verbally abusive, was too proud, and was extremely unpredictable. Complicating issues was the fact that he had the reputation in our community of being an overzealous religious man. He did not take drugs or drink alcohol, to my knowledge and he did work; however, he often could not account for his paycheck. (Years later, while helping him clean up his house, my siblings found many un-cashed checks and cash). My father's lack of organization was a major contributor to our state of poverty. If my mother questioned him about money, his anger would flare. Although he was never physically violent toward us, certainly everything else was fair game. He made life very difficult for his family.

It was not until the fourth grade that I started to realize we were poor. The truth was devastating to me. Once aware, I had an even harder time dealing with my reality. I remember being embarrassed that I received free lunches at school. I would tell people that my parents just prepaid for my meals. Many nights we would go to bed hungry. To comfort us, my mother would say, "Go to sleep and you won't feel hungry." If I were sick, I did not go to a doctor. If I had an earache or sore throat, medicine was not available. My mother would typically say, "Just go to sleep and you'll feel better when you wake up." In retrospect, I cannot imagine what it was like for her to watch her six children suffer with the pain of hunger and sickness.

My mother often quoted us this scripture: **"My God will provide all your needs according to his riches in glory."** (Philippians 4:19). In my experience, I did actually see this scripture come to pass. From grammar school through graduation, I stayed with friends several days a week during the school year. These friends and their families shared their home, food, clothing and love with me. This only confirmed my confidence and faith in Jesus seeing how He used my friends to provide for my needs.

In addition to the poverty, there was also chaos and dysfunction at home. I recall never having clean clothes to wear and always coming home to a dirty house. I do not know if it was because we lived in Florida, but our house was infested with roaches. There were stains on our carpet and our furniture, dirt on our walls, piles of dirty dishes in the sink, and a mountain of dirty laundry piled on the garage floor. I thought our lack of money caused the filth. It was not until I got older that I recognized that poverty did not create the unhealthy living environment; the cause was the dysfunction that existed in my family.

According to my mother, my father grew up in a household that, although wealthy, was clearly dysfunctional. Anything he wanted, my father could have, as long as it was in line with his parent's expectations of him. At the age of ten, my father first discovered and fell in love with "The Beatles." He asked his parents for a guitar which they happily bought for him. They really wanted him to play the trumpet though. They arranged lessons for my father to help him learn to play the trumpet, not the guitar. Unfortunately, my father was not interested. He continued to play the guitar without the support of his parents. My father was always physically strong and he used his strength to intimidate his parents and others in order to get his way. The constant arguing over the guitar versus the trumpet was the fertile soil for the rebellious attitude that grew quite strong within my father. He became prideful and decided that no one would tell him what to do or what not to do. He was angry with his parents for not being supportive of his goals and he holds it against them to this day.

One tragic day, when my father was still a young man, his parents were killed when their private airplane crashed. At the time, his parents were still financially supporting him. Overnight, my father lost all his financial support and was forced to quickly become independent. Unfortunately, he was never able to talk his anger and resentment through with his parents and settle the bitter feelings he harbored toward them which further exacerbated the bad situation.

My parents were married soon after the death of my father's parents. My father held odd jobs. Shortly thereafter, they had twins. Then, two more children were born followed by another set of twins. My father continued to keep picking up employment wherever he could in order to provide for his family of eight.

As I mentioned before, my father was one of those "Jesus Freaks." He was a surfer and loved spending hours at the beach. He would talk to people there about Jesus and pass out tracks (a pamphlet that tells about Jesus). Every Sunday, he took us to church. Outwardly, he appeared to be an exemplary Christian saving his angry outbursts for at home. The hypocrisy was confusing. I do not believe I am alone in this experience. Many of us have seen first-hand those individuals who attend church regularly, speak about God's love, and then behave in a contradictory manner.

My father and I never developed a close relationship. I do not recall much communication between he and any of his children, in fact. As a seven year old, I had fairly severe pain in my knee. Rubbing helped to relieve the pain. I recall wishing that my father would offer to massage the pain away, but I never wanted to ask him. Only one day was I able to find the courage to ask and he did it! He was strong and the pain would go away as long as he was rubbing it. It was not a tender moment at all though; it seemed more like he was carrying out a chore. My knee continued to cause me pain, but I never asked my father to rub it again. I do not ever remember him talking directly to me. His days consisted of going to work, watching the news, eating, and sleeping. If any one of us got too loud and prevented him from hearing the news, he would start yelling at us to be quiet.

As I got older, my father's outbursts were more frequent. I imagine he was concerned about money.

Regardless of the cause, my father seemed to go into a downward spiral having an explosive episode on a daily basis. As children, we learned that when my father came home from work, we needed to scatter like roaches do when the light comes on. We made very sure not get in his line of fire. Usually, our attempts to avoid him were futile. "Kids," he would yell. "Who touched the central air thermostat?" Or, "Who moved my pen? I had a pen sitting right here by the phone. Who moved it? How can I run a business if I can't find a pen to write things down?" He made us come out of hiding to face him, even though none of us were dumb enough to ever touch anything of his. It did not matter that we were not responsible for whatever was causing his anger. He used it as an excuse to have an angry outburst. If he did not like our answers, then things would go flying. He punched through walls and doors. In time, every single bedroom and bathroom door in the house was full of holes. They looked like swiss cheese. Tiles in the bathroom showers were cracked or missing because he had punched them out of frustration. When my father was not having an outburst, he was sitting in his chair in a catatonic state staring straight ahead, lost in his own world.

The most persistent memory I have of my mother is of her sitting in her rocking chair in the living room with her Bible in one hand and a 7/11 big gulp in the other. For what seemed to me to be endless hours in a day, she would sit there reading the Bible and praying. I recall sitting on her lap as she told me stories from the Bible. She would also tell me how much Jesus loved me. My mother was a peaceful woman. I have to give her credit for maintaining her cool while my father continued his violent outbursts. I never remember one single time when my mother yelled at my father; nor did I ever see or hear them fight. My mother's coping mechanism was to walk away from the violence packing her children up and driving us to the park. She would get up out of her chair, gather her little chicks calmly, and load us into the car time after time after time. She did this to protect us from the violence my father was capable of inflicting upon us and I am grateful for her perseverance and protection. I also believe the grace of God protected us by providing the means to get out of the house in time to protect us from the abuse.

I compare my upbringing to a Florida hurricane. Hurricane threats happen often in Florida. As one approaches, families gather and huddle in a closet. Everyone waits in silence trying to hear what is going on outside in order to determine the level of destruction. The most difficult thing about a hurricane is that one never confidently knows when it is over. One brave person has to leave the protected nook to look outside and see if the wind is still blowing or the rain still pouring down. Once the hurricane has passed, everyone comes out of the closet and steps outside to assess the damage. At this moment, there is an unexplainable sense of peace and tranquility. The neighborhood is eerily quiet. The sky is blue and the sun is shining as if nothing ever happened. No one passing through would ever know the danger lurking. That describes my childhood except, of course, the hurricane was my father and damage was his physical destruction of the house and the pain it caused us all emotionally.

It may sound unreasonable that denying a child the right to pursue his love for the guitar could trigger such serious mental problems later in life. I know it is true though because I have seen the effects it had on my father. In fact, the only conversations I have ever had with him are when he has asked me if I liked the songs he had written for the guitar. He is clearly so self-absorbed in his own hurt that he has never even asked me about myself.

Perhaps it would have turned out better for everyone had my father's parents simply accepted and supported his love for the instrument of his choice. My father's parents were maybe wrong to not allow him to pursue his dreams, but I have to believe my father has been wrong all these years to hold it against them. After all, we all make mistakes. Scripture does state that when children obey their parents, they will have a long life on the earth. If my father had obeyed his parents while he was still under their authority, it is very likely that God would have blessed his life and given it a different outcome. He could have waited to pursue his music career or studied both the trumpet and the guitar, but he did not want to submit to his parents and that led him down the wrong path. I believe both parties in this situation chose poorly.

I am not here to point fingers. I am simply using my father's situation as an example of how to better handle conflict. It was through seeing my father's mistakes with his parents, and seeing the truth in the Word of God, that I decided at a young age to obey my parents regardless of the quality of their beliefs and I believe that God has honored that decision by blessing me in many ways with quality of life.

I confess that early in my life, I wanted to change people to be more like myself. I tried to get others to be fighters, like myself. I confronted people and told them that if they were not willing to stand their ground and speak up and do something to improve a situation, then there was something wrong with them. I would wonder, "Why don't they think like me? Why don't they fight like me?" As time went by, the Lord showed me the truth about my dad and my grandparents and the necessity of letting people be who they are. Actually, it is great that we all think differently and have different gifts. When we fail to give the people in our lives free choice, we can have a very negative effect on them.

It is vital for us to understand the importance of allowing people individual freedom of choice. Why is it that God allows us freedom of choice, yet we do not allow others that same freedom? I know it is difficult when we have one conviction in our heart and mind, and someone we love or admire believes differently. It is easy to think that because others do not think like us, they are thinking incorrectly; but this just is not true. In many cases, the opposing party just has a different path to follow. God makes us individuals with different strengths and weaknesses and He gives each of us a different purpose in life. We all need to be more understanding and loving when it comes to those differences. We should not try to change who others are in order to make them who we think they should be. That action can start a chain reaction that leads to destruction as I have witnessed first-hand in my father's life.

Now that my father's parents have passed away, he could still have peace by giving the pain and anger that remains unresolved between he and his parents to God. It is never too late. I have prayed for years that my father would truly let go of his anger and I believe that he has made progress. Matthew 6:14-15 states, **"For if you forgive men when they sin against you, your Heavenly Father will also forgive you. But if you do not forgive men their sins, your Father will not forgive your sins."** 1 John 1:9 says, **"If we confess our sins, he is faithful and just and will forgive us our sins and purify us from all unrighteousness."** If you have had someone leave your life without resolving the conflict or the hurt they caused you, I urge you to forgive them now. It can only improve your situation and your future.

I am truly blessed because I had a mother who instilled in me at a very young age that Jesus loves me. That knowledge helped safeguard my heart, believing that no matter what unreasonable and potentially damaging choices and actions my parents presented to me, I had Jesus by my side. Knowing that I was loved unconditionally, made it much easier to avoid ever believing I was a victim regardless of how severely mistreated I was by my father.

I know that there are millions of people who have experienced abusive parenting. I am telling you this story to let you know that you are not alone. We have a God that knew our name before we were even conceived. The Bible tells us that, **"He knows how many hairs we have on our head."** (Matthew 10:30). He loves us more than we could ever imagine.

Relative to my father, I was forced to question whether it was possible for a person to love God, to know the words of the Bible, to tell others about Him, and still have serious emotional problems. Because of my father, I have to believe it is possible. Eventually, his choices and ways of thinking translated into my wrong ways of thinking. Most mindsets, or what I will call, "templates" are established from our environment or circumstances. The way we think becomes our reality, even though it may not be based upon truth. It is so important to reflect upon our life and ask God if we have any wrong templates that we created at a young age.

When God started showing me things about my father, I knew His purpose was to indicate to me how I was demonstrating similar traits. I started to understand how I needed to revise my ways of thinking. I began to see that I had anger issues and I did not trust God. Just like my father, I felt the need to fight about everything. I was angry at God and did not trust Him to take care of me in life because I looked around at my surroundings and could not see Him there. I did not fully understand that 1) God uses trials to teach us about ourselves and Himself and 2) that He is always with us, whether we believe it or not. Of course, being a natural fighter and physically strong like my father did not help the situation. The secret is to learn at a young age how to submit to authority and to know that God always dearly loves us, and that God never, ever leaves us alone.

One time when my mother was removing us from harms way, I started to get a fire inside of me. I had this yearning to take charge and fight. I felt confident that I could defeat my father and I was not feeling afraid of him. I remember feeling so frustrated that my mother would not stay and confront him for his horrible behavior. "Why do we always have to leave?" I objected.

My namesake is General Robert E. Lee who was a direct ancestor of my mother's favorite uncle, George Lee. She loved him so much she wanted to name a child after him. My older brother was born and he was named after my father. When I was born, she named me Lee Cassia. She was right in naming me after a general. It stands to reason that it was very difficult for me to passively watch my mom give up and leave. She was smart though because she knew that I would have stepped up to fight against my father and would have been caught in the cross fire of his rage if she had not removed me from the house.

There was another incident when my mother was driving us away and my dad came out of the house chasing us and throwing lawn furniture at the car. This was just a typical day at our house. Yet every Sunday we would all go to church together and act like everything was fine. The only daily communication with our father was when he would ask us as we were going to bed; "Kids, did you read the Bible today?" Meanwhile, the smell of fresh drywall mud lingered in the air - one of many recent patch-up jobs to hide my father's most recent violent episode. Here I was, a child living in an environment where one parent is violent while professing to be a Christian while another parent spends all day talking to God yet consistently runs away from her problems. As I got a little older, I began asking myself, "Who do I want to be? What templates have I created in order to simply cope with the dysfunction that has been all around me? What do I need to change?'

      What templates have you created in your life? The only way you will ever be able to change your life is if you decide to allow the Holy Spirit to make the necessary changes. The only way your life will change is if you face life head on. Do not ever be ashamed if you have made mistakes. My father never wanted to admit any of his mistakes. He would always blame someone or something else. Again, I am telling you about him so you can see that he had a choice, I also had a choice, and we all have a choice. We have to realize God's love for us and we have to trust Him. We can choose to become a victim or we can move ourselves away from that, take responsibility, and make the choice to overcome our adversities. I could have easily felt victimized due to the abusive household I grew up in; however, I chose to learn how to trust God instead and focus on His love for me. We cannot do both. We cannot see ourselves as a victim and fully understand that God loves us. The two ways of thinking conflict.

Chapter 3
Discovering My Template

When we are young, we develop templates which are really just tendencies to act, think, and believe a certain way. These templates are formed in part by our natural ability and personality. Also influencing the development of our templates is our environment; the way of life around us. In Psychology, we learn to call this "Nature vs. Nurture."

I am naturally both a confident and fearless person; however, I believe that my environment transformed me into a fighter. I have always been very strong physically and when I combine my physical strength with my strong willpower, I can become a great warrior. The problem is that I did not always know how and when to use those natural gifts correctly. Because of the erratic behavior, angry personalities, and dysfunction that I experienced as a child, I grew up misguided as to how to properly use my strengths.

God gives each one of us supernatural and natural gifts and abilities. Just as an athlete with natural athletic abilities has to train and develop their gifts, we too, as Christians, have to develop the gifts that God has given us.

For me, my gifts were the traits associated with those of a lion. If untrained and underdeveloped, I could cause massive destruction like that of my father.

My need to protect others began as a child. I would get so angry with mother for not standing up to my father. In retrospect, I am sure my mother did what she thought was best for everyone involved, but I wanted her to fight against the injustice my father was inflicting upon us and she would not. My frustration began to develop a certain way of thinking. I began formulating a template in my mind that defined how I would act if I ever saw anyone being mistreated, I would fight to protect them. I wanted every person who mistreated another person to be held accountable; particularly if they called themselves a Christian. Personally, I came to see myself as a lion and a warrior who never again wanted to be victimized.

Heading into my freshman year of high school, I still had this thought that I was not going to tolerate any type of abuse. If I saw any level of mistreatment, I would not just walk away. Instead, I would confront it.

That year I went on a trip to Helen, Georgia with my German Club. One day during the trip, I was with my friends in our hotel room. A friend was just getting out of the shower when I heard a knock on the door. I went over to answer the door and was greeted by six senior girls. One student barged in and started yelling at my friend who had just come out of the shower and was wrapped in a towel. In a flash, the girl punched my friend. I thought to myself, "That did not just happen!" The girl who swung the punch ran out the door. I ran and caught up with her. She was standing with her friends for protection. In my mind, I had been telling myself for years, "Attack. Attack. Protect the weak." There was no stopping me. I thought, "I'll take them all on. I'm stronger than all of them put together." In fact, I had just set the record for the strongest bench press in the entire high school.

One of the girls started swinging her compact at me. With one swing with my left hook, she was down. Just as I was about to go after the rest of the girls, a football player threw me over his shoulder and removed me from the situation.

Things calmed down and we all headed back to Florida. Upon our return to school, I had to go to the Principal's office. I was protecting my friend and felt that my actions were justified. The Principal did not agree and I was suspended for three days. For the rest of my high school years, I bore the nick-name, "Rocky."

I had a hard time knowing how to react in situations if I saw someone being treated unjustly. I did not want to be passive like my mother, nor did I want to be violent like my father. God was about to send trials my way in order to help me overcome my incorrect ways of thinking and my tendency to react angrily. The Lord was going to use trials to teach me how and when to protect people in His way. He was going to use my circumstances to turn me from a lion into a lamb.

I obviously failed the first trial as well as many more afterwards. Changing a template is a difficult task because it becomes a deeply set pattern in our mind and heart. It becomes even harder for those of you who are master justifiers like myself. I always had a great reason why I acted the way I did; after all, I was just protecting the weak. What was incorrect about my thinking was how I always felt it was my responsibility to protect people and how I believed violence would correct violence. This is how my lack of trust in God became more evident to me. I knew that God loved me; however, I did not trust Him to vindicate either myself or others. I did not practice the scripture that states in Psalm 4:2, **"O God, my vindicator! Answer me when I call! When I was distressed, you set me free; now have mercy on me, and hear my prayer."**

One time my family and I were at an arcade playing when this older man walked over to my teenage brother and started harassing him. So what did I do? I got in his face, of course. I should have just led my brother away from the situation instead of getting face to face with the man, but I wanted to fight him. I wanted to prove to myself that I was going to protect the weak at all cost. It was only by God's mercy and grace that the man did not hit me. Fortunately, we eventually walked away from the situation without a physical altercation. My template was all wrong.

So, how was I able to get rid of this wrong template and change? Was it an overnight change? Do you think I asked others to pray for me? No! Remember I am strong willed which is really just a nice word for stubborn. It took another trial.

When I was a teenager, I worked at my uncle's restaurant. I saw my uncle speaking to his daughter-in-law in a mean and condescending manner. Of course, I stepped in between them and asked him if there was a problem. He looked at me, decided it was not worth his time, and walked away. Again, I unwisely stepped into the line of fire of an uncle who also had an explosive temper, just like his brother, my father. I am not saying that I was wrong to come to my cousin-in-law's aid, but there is a right way and a wrong way to handle conflict. I was still learning.

In my early twenties, I worked at a restaurant in NYC. The manager lacked good management skills. He would yell at the servers and call them names in front of the customers. He also never paid us for work we did. So one night after he yelled at a server, I refused to let it go on any longer. I did not get violent or even approach him this time. I knew he would react poorly to any intervention. Instead, I convinced half of the servers to walk out during our shift. I realized that I did not have to use violence to stand up for someone and I did not have to confront the person face to face. Instead, I convinced everyone to go to the Department of Labor and make a claim against him for not paying us our wages. All of the servers followed my lead. The outcome was that he was fined and required to pay all of us our wages. I know he will never forget me.

It may seem as if I finally learned a safe and effective means to accomplish my goal. Well, partially correct. I was able to revise the need to fight people and get in their faces; however, I still had a bold, blunt, and strong personality that needed to be toned down and I still had hidden anger lying deep inside and I did not trust God to take care of everything.

One time when I was much older, my father went into one of his tirades and said he was going to kill himself. He pushed me out of his way. Nobody pushes me without consequence and nobody is ever going to kill himself on my watch. After he pushed me, I grabbed him, threw him to the ground, and put him in a chokehold. I did not start punching him. Instead, with my hands still on him, I started praying out loud for him. Just like in Matthew 18:18, **"Verily I say unto you, Whatsoever ye shall bind on earth shall be bound in heaven: and whatsoever ye shall loose on earth shall be loosed in heaven."** I was binding Satan's attack against my father. I recalled scriptures like Luke 10:19**, "Behold! I have given you authority and power to trample upon serpents and scorpions, and [physical and mental strength and ability] over all the power that the enemy [possesses]; and nothing shall in any way harm you."** There was no way humanly possible that I could have overtaken my father with my strength alone. I am very strong, but my father is much stronger. I was beginning to learn how to fight God's way. Instantly, peace came upon both of us and my father was calm again.

Nowadays, my father knows I will not tolerate his belligerent behavior. Anytime he starts to get agitated, I look at him and he stops. In the situation above, my bold, fearless, and courageous personality was finally put to good use. I was slowly starting to see when and how to effectively behave like a lion.

God makes us all a certain way. He instills characteristics in each of us and teaches us how to keep them in check and balance. I was starting to allow God to train and develop my gifts. Could you imagine what might have happened had I tried that tactic on my boss at the restaurant? Every situation is different and requires prayer and seeking God's wisdom. We need to allow God to show us any wrong templates we have created and how to overcome them.

Chapter 4
Correcting My Template

Growing up in a dysfunctional home affected how I reacted to stressful situations. My mother did not know how to handle my father's rage and she developed multiple avoidance tactics. As children traumatized by violence in our home, we all developed a strong, but false need to protect others. I never considered protecting my brothers and sisters to be a bad thing until I became an adult. It was then I realized that the way I protected my siblings was actually hurting them and pushing them away.

As an adult, I reacted to situations in my adult life the same way I would have as a child. I thought I had to be aggressive. I had to be strong, bold, and confident. I had to protect the weak. I had to be a lion - not a lioness, but a lion. Even though I am a female, every vision I had of myself was of a lion. It has to do with my hair. When I would see my reflection, I would picture a lion's thick mane. People to this day will comment that my hair looks like a lion's mane. My hair is only one characteristic of a lion that God has given to me. I trusted in my natural ability to protect others and really did believe that it was up to me to protect others, particularly my siblings. This is where my lack of trusting God began.

During a college break, I decided to go live with my sister. She said I could live with her without charge and she helped me find employment by directing me towards an opening at a daycare facility. She offered to let me work and save all of my money for the following semester. I gratefully accepted her offer. It was a hard time though. We shared a tiny bedroom in a three-bedroom apartment with two other housemates. I slept on the floor on an egg crate. Everything I owned at that point in my life fit into one suitcase. I did not have a car, so I had to rely on my sister to transport me to and from work. Even though it was a tough living situation, I was glad that I had my sister there to help me save the money necessary to be able to return to school.

This is an example of how we protected and took care of each other. Even though my sister is older and helped me out financially, I always felt like I was the one who needed to protect her. She has a big heart. She has always loved the Lord and is intent on pleasing and obeying Him. That sounds like a positive quality, but it can become a negative characteristic if one becomes a people pleaser and cannot say no to people which is exactly what I saw happening with her.

I thought I needed to protect her from people who misused her. It started with her roommates. I was planning on staying for two months until the fall semester started. One of the roommates had her own bathroom and a room three times larger than ours. The other roommate's bedroom was twice as large. The roommates had their boyfriends spending the night. One boyfriend practically lived there. One day my sister confronted me and said that the roommates wanted me to start paying rent. I knew that my sister would just agree with them. I felt the lion in me was getting ready to pounce. When we gathered together in the living room to discuss the issue, I said, "No way will I pay rent when your boyfriends stay over all the time and we have the smallest room. If you want, I will help pay the utility bills." Luckily, they agreed and the issue was settled.

I continued to feel the constant need to protect my family. Unfortunately, I got myself into all kinds of trouble thinking I had to solve everything on my own. All of the trials I will share with you happened in my twenties and early thirties before I was able to recognize the error of my ways. Eventually, I was able to mellow. I will always be a strong person, but the Lord helped me to transform into a gentler lamb.

Chapter 5
Correcting With Love

    My habit was to confront people in order to protect those around me and challenge them in order to hold them accountable for their actions. My attitude caused many trials and mistakes. We do have the right to hold people accountable for their actions; but only with God's guidance. If we decide to approach another in hope of bringing awareness of wrong behavior, this absolutely has to be done out of love and with the application of God's wisdom and guidance from the Holy Spirit. Without loving correction, a person will not be able to receive the words properly.

    As someone who is very bold, blunt, and to the point, I especially had to revise my approach. Some people are like lambs, and if approached like a lion, they can feel devoured instead of helped. This is why it is so important to be able to allow God to change us. In contrast, some people are like lambs and God is trying to change them into more of a lion. Our approach should depend in part on our audience. As Paul stated in I Corinthians 9:20, **"To the Jews I became like a Jew, to win the Jews. To those** under the law I became like one under the law (though I myself am not under the law,) so as to win those under the law. To those not having the law I became like one not having the law (though I am not free from God's law but am under Christ's law), so as to win those not having the law. To the weak I became weak, to win the weak. I have become all things to all people so that by all possible means I might save some."** God's intent is not to take away what He created us to be; He simply wants to add more dimension to our makeup.

The above scripture made me realize that I needed to learn how to become weak in order to help the weak. I needed to learn how to hone my lion-like traits so that I could effectively help people without harming them. It is impossible to help others unless one is able to relate to their characteristics. Not all people are strong, confident, and bold in character.

I will share an example of how another person, with a lion-like disposition, corrected me. Because the rebuke was not offered in love, it was very hard for me to receive the words and make the needed changes. Correction should always be offered lovingly regardless of our natural tendency to yell, argue, control, or get upset. A lion, unlike a lamb, is not known for its gentleness. Unfortunately I did not discover this wisdom until after I had failed repeatedly.

When I was twenty three years old, I was sitting in church and the pastor called people up to the front who needed prayer. A huge crowd went forward and there were more people in need of prayer than there were leaders in the church to pray. Before that time, I had never prayed aloud for anyone aside from family members. I noticed one of my friends standing alone. Right away I heard the Lord say, "Go and pray with her for unity." Now when the Lord speaks to me, it is not a loud thunderous voice coming from heaven. It is my voice I hear, but it is more of a peaceful quiet voice. My heart started to race with fear but then I asked myself, "Okay, she's my friend. I'm in church. What could possibly go wrong?" I know some of you are asking, "This girl took on a New York City restaurant owner and tackled her own father to the ground and now she's afraid to pray out loud?" Yes, I was.

    The Lord was taking me out of my comfort zone. He was dealing with me on this issue. He kept telling me, "Words have power. You need to speak them aloud." I thought about the scripture in Matthew 18:19-20 that states, **"Again, truly I tell you that if two of you on earth agree about anything they ask for, it will be done for them by my Father in heaven. For where two or three gather in my name, there am I with them."** I needed to get over my fear of praying with people. I told myself, "Just go up there and do what the Lord told you to do!"

    One of the important lessons to learn here is that we never know what God is teaching someone and we never know another's weaknesses. It is not enough to start looking at ourselves through God's eyes; we must look at others through His eyes as well. We need to ask ourselves before we speak to someone, "I wonder what God is doing in their life?" The whole point of life is that God wants to get rid of our fleshly thoughts and characteristics to make room for His righteous thoughts and Godly characteristics. I find myself wondering, "What trial is someone else going through right now?" What characteristic of God is He trying to demonstrate for this person?"

    I finally went up to my friend and asked, "What do you need prayer for?"

    She said, "Please pray for my husband's protection."

Her husband was in the service overseas. Now here is where I made a rookie mistake because of fear. I told her that the Lord wanted me to pray for something else. I totally ignored her request and continued with my unity prayer.

That night the friend I prayed with called me and let me have it. I felt like I had been hit by a semi-truck. She was screaming, "Who do you think you are, not to pray for what I asked?" She was relentless in her attack reducing me to tears. I was sobbing and said repeatedly, "I'm sorry. I'm sorry." You would think that would have been the end of that, but it was not. The next day I got a call from the youth pastor. He wanted to meet with both of us. Of course, I agreed to meet. I was so scared and felt so hurt that I asked my sister to come with me. Miss bold, strong, fearless lion was petrified. Upon meeting, my friend started yelling at me again. Again, I began crying and asking for her forgiveness. After that, we never spoke again.

Did my friend have a valid point? Yes, of course she did. However, did she handle it correctly? No, I do not believe she did because she did not correct me out of love. It is a good thing that I am a lion and that it takes a lot to knock me down. That experience could have scared me enough to stop me from ever reaching out to others with prayer again. However, I chose to learn from my mistake and to move forward. I refused to feel victimized or inhibited by the experience. When a fellow believer comes up to us and steps out in faith, even if they make a mistake, we can feel honored that God is allowing us to, lovingly, correct the person and help them walk in their faith and grow.

There are several lessons I learned from this experience. First of all, I took a wrong approach in how I prayed. My friend requested a prayer that was on her heart.

I should have recognized her request and then followed with what God had put on my heart to pray for her.

In addition, violence can come in the form of verbal attack and I was guilty. In the past, I corrected people in the same unruly manner as my friend did with me. What is the point of correcting people if they do not receive it? What is the point of bring awareness to someones wrong actions if it intimidates that person in the process? If I had to learn how to be a lamb in order to help another grow and change, then why would I refuse that change? I already knew how to be a lion. I wanted to learn how to be all things to all people so that I could help them.

I had to learn the hard way how to best confront someone on an issue that needed to be addressed. Through trials such as the incident praying for a friend, we learn what is important and little by little become more like God. It is vitally important to allow God the opportunity to develop the gifts He has given us through trial and error, different experiences, and sheer obedience. That is how we receive peace, which in turn, produces faith, hope, and love.

Next, as Christians, we need to understand that every person is always in the process of learning. We are on a path that takes us from glory to glory, meaning our goal in life is to become more and more like Jesus every day. The process never ends until we are in heaven.

I began to wonder if it was better to practice using my gifts and what I felt God was prompting me to do with Christians versus Non-Christians. Sometimes we have to just step out in faith and try out an idea. How else are we to know if we are hearing from God correctly? My fear was that if I were to practice on non-believers, that I might detour them from salvation if my actions were incorrect. Many non-believers tell me they are not Christians because of something a Christian did to them. Concerning developing our God given gifts or trying to hear from God, I think it best to go to fellow Christians. A Christian will generally have more patience with another. Church is the perfect place to practice our gifts and learn how to hear from God because other Christians are aware of the growth process.

Finally, we must fix our eyes on Jesus and His love for us and on His teachings. Unless we are free from a victim mentality, we will never fully develop into the person God meant us to be. If we allow our problems to be all-consuming, we will never be able to see the answer. We have to be okay with making mistakes, knowing that we can learn from them. We have to be able to let our thoughts and emotions go in order to receive more from God.

It was not until lately that I finally learned how to become a lamb and learned how to confront people out of love. I still make mistakes, but fortunately, I am quicker to repent and correct my actions. It has taken me 36 years to become a tamed lion. In the past, my reckless modus operandi just did not work. As a result, the people I was trying to correct did not receive the information. I pushed people farther away from the truth and acted viciously out of control. That was all I knew. That was how I survived; fight, be strong, and protect others at all costs. Fortunately, God was working in my life to change how I thought. He was teaching me that my wrong way of thinking impacted my life in a negative way and negatively affected those around me.

Chapter 6
Misplaced Convictions

I was in my early twenties when my older sister graduated with her Master's degree and was offered a great position in Connecticut. She accepted the job and relocated. I wanted to be able to go back to school the following semester, but was unable to afford both living accommodations and save for tuition. Again my sister extended an invitation to live with her for free so I could save. So I moved to Connecticut. Initially, living with her was great. Even though it was a tiny apartment and I was back to sleeping on the floor on a thin egg crate again, we got along well, as usual. We would go to church several times a week and were highly involved in church activities.

At first, I did not recognize the problem with our routine. My sister helped me get a job at the pharmaceutical company where she was employed. Things seemed good. I did not feel like I needed to protect her as the previous year and I felt that she was really helping me. We relocated to a larger apartment where I was able to have my own room and a bed - a welcomed change.

At that time, my younger sister was showing an interest in singing. She told me that the Lord was telling her she was going to be a singer. I spoke to my older sister and asked her if our younger sister could move in with us to be closer to NYC and, of course, she approved. Taking care of each other and protecting each other was the standard with which we were raised. Shortly thereafter, my younger sister moved in with us and it was not until then that I realized I had always done what my older sister wanted. I had stopped doing the things I enjoyed. For the very first time in my life, I began to realize the importance of being different and thinking differently. I felt a new freedom to be my own person.

God has made us all unique. We need to realize that just because we feel convicted about something does not mean that everyone else has to have the same conviction. If someone does not share that same belief, it does not mean that the other person is wrong. God made us individuals with different gifts and purposes. He equips us with what we are going to need in order to finish our race. 1 Corinthians 9:24-26 reads; **"Do you not know that in a race all the runners run, but only one gets the prize? Run in such a way as to get the prize. Everyone who competes in the games goes into strict training. They do it to get a crown that will not last, but we do it to get a crown that will last forever. Therefore I do not run like someone running aimlessly; I do not fight like a boxer beating the air. No, I strike a blow to my body and make it my slave so that after I have preached to others, I myself will not be disqualified for the prize."**

Not all of us are going to train the same. Not all of us are going to be running in the same race. We need to be careful about the beliefs we force upon others. As long as we are standing firm in our own convictions, we do not need to worry about someone else's convictions. 1 Corinthians 8:7-13 states, **"But not everyone possesses**

this knowledge. Some people are still so accustomed to idols that when they eat sacrificial food they think of it as having been sacrificed to a god, and since their conscience is weak, it is defiled. But food does not bring us near to God; we are no worse if we do not eat, and no better if we do. Be careful, however, that the exercise of your rights does not become a stumbling block to the weak. For if someone with a weak conscience sees you, with all your knowledge, eating in an idol's temple, won't that person be emboldened to eat what is sacrificed to idols? So this weak brother or sister, for whom Christ died, is destroyed by your knowledge. When you sin against them in this way and wound their weak conscience, you sin against Christ. Therefore, if what I eat causes my brother or sister to fall into sin, I will never eat meat again, so that I will not cause them to fall." I will speak more about this scripture in the paragraphs to come.

Where I grew up in Florida, there were all-age nightclubs where teenagers could dance. I absolutely loved the ability to go out dancing at a young age. I have always felt that I was born to dance, almost as if that is what God created me to do. At the dance clubs, I danced for Him. I could always feel Him smiling down on me.

I also loved to go to the movies and when my younger sister arrived she would go dancing and to the movies with me. My older sister would never want to go. My younger sister and I would ask our older sister if she wanted to go to the movies and she would decline because she believed movies were a bad influence. We would also ask her to go to the mall with us and she would decline because she felt overwhelmed there. Eventually we just stopped asking her to join us. If she did not want to go, she did not have to.

It is very important that you do not let your convictions become doctrine. In other words, just because you think something is wrong, it does not mean that it is wrong for everyone. Some people believe it is wrong, if you can imagine this, for women to wear pants, cut their hair, or play cards. Each person needs to find their own balance and comfort level and our job is to be accepting of individual convictions and beliefs, within reason.

The same goes for faith. Because everyone's faith is on a different level, there is no "catch-all" list of faith rules. God gives us each faith for our specific need, as He has made us individuals and deals with each one of us on an individual basis. We each have a specific destiny and God uses things in our lives to help us reach our individual calling.

There are specific sins listed in the Bible that we are to refrain from; however, there are also some things that are left to be settled between each person and God. That is why it is important to have a relationship with the Holy Spirit who is the being that places those convictions on our hearts. You know that feeling you get inside that says, "Not a good idea" or "Yes, go for it?" That is what I am talking about. Some refer to it as a gut feeling or that they, "just know what to do." Not everyone will have the same convictions with certain things and the range of topics is enormous. Romans 14:23 reads, **"But if you have doubts about whether or not you should eat something, you are sinning if you go ahead and do it. For you are not following your convictions. If you do anything you believe is not right, you are sinning."** This implies that sin can be simply acting or thinking in opposition to a personal belief. My younger sister and I respected our other sister's convictions. Through my relationship with her, I eventually came to understand the principle of accepting differences.

To return to the subject of dance, I cannot remember a time when I was not dancing. When I was eleven years old, I made a dance video with my younger brother and sister. I felt like a star. At the age of twelve, a whole new world of dancing opened up to me when the show "In Living Color" came to television. Featured on this show was the dance team called, "Fly Girls." Before a commercial break, they would come out and do a dance routine. I would sit and watch them dance and try to learn their routine. I was in such awe. Then, I saw a music video of Janet Jackson, "Rhythm Nation." I dreamed of being her back up dancer.

By the time I was sixteen, I spent every weekend in the nightclubs. I remember the experience of arriving with my friends and then hearing the rhythm of the music, blocking everything out, and dancing for hours. I know it might sound crazy, but I would dance for the Lord. When I would dance, I would think of His love for me and that made dancing even more delightful. In all the years of going to nightclubs, I never danced with a guy. In all the years of going to nightclubs, I never took one sip of alcohol. I did not know it at the time, but God was teaching me how to be a light in a dark world. **"If you were of the world, the world would love you as its own; but because you are not of the world, but I chose you out of the world, therefore the world hates you."** (John 15:19). I never succumbed to the worldly practices of the nightclub scene. **"Do not conform any longer to the pattern of this world, but be transformed by the renewing of your mind. Then you will be able to test and approve what God's will is - his good, pleasing and perfect will."** (Romans 12:2).

I am not sure how old I was, maybe nineteen, when my younger sister and I went to a dance club and heard they were having a dance contest. We both looked at each other and said, "Let's do it." We entered the competition and I remember to this day the announcers saying our names. We went up on the stage and I felt that the presence of the Lord was with me. We both wanted to dance our hearts out for God. We went up on stage and without having practiced a routine, my sister and I somehow managed to dance in perfect synchronicity. We did not win the contest, but the experience reinforced the desire in my heart to want to reach the destiny that God had for me. I wanted to make sure that every time I went to a dance club, I would dance for the Lord. I wanted to be a light in a dark world. Every time I went dancing, I would jump up on the huge speakers in the clubs and dance on them. It was great because no one would bother me up there.

I loved it when my younger sister would go dancing with me. She was the only one who understood what I was doing at the clubs. She also loved the Lord with all her heart and loved to dance. It was sad because going to the nightclubs was the only time, aside from at home, that my sister and I could dance freely for the Lord. One time when we were in a club, we started praying, "God, move through us like a train." Then, all at once, the DJ started playing a beat that sounded like a train. I believe God was preparing us not to let worldliness influence us, but rather, to allow us to influence the world around us.

When God calls a person into a ministry, or a profession for a religion, He may do so in a way that does not line up with what the church is used to seeing or believing. Most Christians would assume that a nightclub would not be a place that God could use as a place to teach a person about Himself. I knew my own innocence, however, and danced in clubs for almost fifteen years without ever getting involved with another man or alcohol. Please, I am not saying that if you are a Christian and go to a club, dance with a man, or drink alcohol that you are a bad person. I just want to clarify my intentions; I danced for the Lord only. I would focus on Him.

    We have to be careful about what convictions we push on other people or Christians because we never really know what God is teaching that person. It is unfair to push our convictions on people as if our convictions are doctrines. I knew that I had the ability to go to clubs and not disappoint God. At the same time, I would never tell any of my Christian friends that it was okay to do what I did as their faith may have differed from mine.

    One summer when I came home for a college break, I asked my two friends, who had always gone dancing with me in the past, if they wanted to go again. They both were in agreement and one said, "No, we are committing our lives to the Lord." What struck me as funny was that I was the one always praying for them and encouraging them to live for the Lord. Now they were telling me not to go dancing, so I asked the Lord about it. He said, "What is not of faith is sin. If they do not have faith to go to the clubs and use it as an opportunity to be a light, then do not pressure them to go. However, they should not push their convictions upon you." That was when the Lord started teaching me about this concept of a personal faith. My friends had no idea where my heart was when I would go to the clubs. I knew I was doing the right thing for myself.

    I had all the faith necessary to go to the nightclubs and be a light without falling short of who God wanted me to be. Others might fall into temptation, just like the scripture 1 Corinthians 8:7-13, **"But not everyone** possesses this knowledge. Some people are still so accustomed to idols that when they eat sacrificial food they think of it as having been sacrificed to a god, and since their conscience is weak, it is defiled. But food does not bring us near to God; we are no worse if we do not eat, and no better if we do. Be careful, however, that the exercise of your rights does not become a stumbling block to the weak. For if someone with a weak conscience sees you, with all your knowledge, eating in an idol's temple, won't that person be emboldened to eat what is sacrificed to idols? So this weak brother or sister, for whom Christ died, is destroyed by your knowledge. When you sin against them in this way and wound their weak conscience, you sin against Christ. Therefore, if what I eat causes my brother or sister to fall into sin, I will never eat meat again, so that I will not cause them to fall."

My friends did not have the same calling on their life that I had. It was only a few years later, when the Lord called my sister to be a singer in the secular industry. That was when it hit me: God always sends his disciples out by twos. He told me that all of those times we went dancing and prayed at the clubs, our prayers were breaking Satan's hold on the music industry. We were planting seeds with our prayers. We were exhibiting righteous behavior. We were showing people that they can go out and have fun without getting themselves into a compromising situation. We were showing people that we do not have to dance provocatively or use drugs or alcohol to have a good time. In the process, we were laying the necessary groundwork for what would become my sister's ministry and career: ground work that would help her go out into the world and be a light without falling into the temptation of fame and greed and a life displeasing to God. We were also preparing our hearts and laying a good, strong foundation that would be hard to break when she, a lamb, was surrounded by wolves.

One day I know that my younger sister is going to be on a stage at the national level. The Lord is going to use her dancing and singing to bring glory to Himself. I know that we fought and won many battles in the entertainment industry. It is through all of those years of preparation that I have grown confident that God is faithful to complete His works.

Chapter 7
Drawing My Sword

During the time when my two sisters and I were all living together, one of them started going to a new church. With this sister, I knew that if I wanted to have a relationship with her, I would have to join her wherever she went. I was okay with following her choices as I still felt responsible for protecting her.

I began attending this new church with her. Six months was all I could handle. It took me no time at all to see that the church programs were ineffective. The things that were being preached were not completely true. Matthew 7:15-16 states, **"Beware of false prophets, who come to you in sheep's clothing, but inwardly they are ravenous wolves. You will know them by their fruits. Do men gather grapes from thorn bushes or figs from thistles?"** The words I was hearing did not line up with the Word of God and that was of great concern to me. To give an example, the pastor told my sister that God told him that she should marry his best friend, so my sister did. The pastor led his people from his congregation to a gravesite where an old prophet was buried to try to raise his spirit up and ask from it guidance. The pastor's wife had an affair which resulted in divorce. The pastor changed his church's name and location several times over a short period of time. The church exuded a sense of chaos and confusion and I wanted to have nothing to do with it.

The craziness continued. My sister and her husband were heavily influenced by this supposed man of God. He told my brother-in-law to turn down a job offer in order to create more time for his family and the two then proceeded to play video games while my sister went to work to support their family. At the pastor's suggestion, they all relocated to another state, then shortly afterwards moved back again with his prompting. The pastor had complete control over my sister. She believed whatever he said and would not accept the truth of Matthew 7 that a pastor could, in fact, be wrong and dangerously misleading.

I went into protective mode. You would think that I would have learned by now the correct way to respond to trials. However, as we all know, it is easy to revert back to our old habits. I kept thinking about all of these scriptures: **"For false messiahs and false prophets will appear and perform great signs and wonders to deceive, if possible, even the elect."** (Matthew 24:24) **"But there were also false prophets among the people, just as there will be false teachers among you. They will secretly introduce destructive heresies, even denying the sovereign Lord who bought them--bringing swift destruction on themselves."** (2 Peter 2:1). **"And many false prophets will appear and will deceive many people."** (Matthew 24:11).

I know it is not always wise to judge a pastor; however, this scripture gave me the green light. I was upset by the negative influence this man was having on my sister's life. In the past, she was able to offer inspired words to others who were clearly touched by what she shared. My sister, who was once so filled with the Holy Spirit and sensitive to His guidance, now could barely remember she used to be like that. This is the same sister who was once so strongly convicted to avoid the mall and movies with me. Now was doing all of the things she previously stood adamantly against with this pastor and his wife. I no longer saw the fruit in her life that was clearly evident before she was involved with her new church. In fact, she was becoming unrecognizable. I already knew the importance of not forcing my beliefs on someone else and so I faced a dilemma. Should I share my personal convictions with her, or not?

    I knew that my sister had strong beliefs about certain things. When I saw her heading off to the movies within one month of meeting this pastor and his wife, I recognized that her need to people please had gone into overdrive. The pastor did not know my sister, or her convictions and I falsely felt it was my duty to protect her and keep her on track. Being my bold self, I addressed the issue with her. I asked her directly why she was suddenly doing things with this person that she had never done before. I asked her how her beliefs could change overnight. She eluded my questions and ignored my concerns and continued to participate in their lives against her own previously held convictions.

    So, what do you think I did? I started confronting her increasingly in my usual bold hurtful way. I was not asking God how I was supposed to confront her. My intensions did not include being loving or trying to relate. I just went into attack mode. I fully believe that everything I was telling her was correct, but I was approaching the issues like a bulldozer ridding a pile of rubble. I was acting just like my friend who corrected me about how I prayed with her. My strong templates, my patterns of thinking and behaving kicked in. I needed to protect the weak. I needed to protect my family and not just run away from situations as I saw my mother do repeatedly. I thought to myself, "Bring out your sword and fight" and that is how I handled that particular conflict.

At that time, I did not fully understand the scripture I mentioned earlier in 1 Corinthians 9 about how best to assist the weak. One must almost become weak to be able to help the weak. Eventually, I saw how my reactions were incorrect and how I, even with the best of intentions, had made matters worse instead of better.

There were issues with another sister as well. She had to have a kidney transplant. One day when we were driving to the hospital to take her children to visit her after her surgery, my nephew started hitting me and being very aggressive towards me in the car. I could not understand what was going on. My mother was in the car and asked him why he was hitting me. He said that he had to fight the bad guys. We had no idea what he was talking about. It was not until later when my mother made the connection. At the time my nephew loved to watch E.T. and was living out the scene when E.T. was taken to the hospital and the doctors were doing all kinds of tests on him. During this scene the boy, Elliott, was screaming to the doctors, "You're hurting him!" At the time, my nephew was only two years old. He has never had his mommy taken away from him and held in a hospital. My mother and I came to realize that he thought his mother was in trouble and that the doctors were hurting her, just like in E.T. He thought they were the bad guys. He was ready to fight to protect his mother and was simply expressing his aggression and fear by hitting me.

The Lord used this as an example for me. He showed me how I also had the wrong enemy in mind. Like my nephew, who thought the doctors were the enemy, I thought this pastor was the enemy. I thought I had to confront him and all of his wrong actions, that it was my responsibility.

I also saw how my nephew was fighting me instead of the real enemy. Likewise, I was about to attack the wrong person. Instead of attacking Satan and his evil devices, I was attacking people. That is what I mean by saying I was still set in the wrong template. I was still fighting situations the same way as if I were a child. I needed to grow up and realize people have their differences and the battle is, ultimately, the Lord's.

It is amazing to me how even though we have awful things happen to us, we act out those same behaviors towards others. I remember always thinking about how the Israelites had to travel forty years on an eleven day journey because they kept making the same mistakes over and over. They kept complaining and not trusting God. I would always ask, "Lord, why wouldn't they listen? Why wouldn't they just do what you asked and get it over with?" Well, now I know why. I did the exact same thing. The Lord was always dealing with me on my presentation. He would say, "Cassia, what you are saying is correct but how you are saying it is incorrect." What good does it do to have wisdom if people cannot receive it from you? It was not until this next event that happened in my life that I began to realize the severe consequences of disobeying God. Only two people out of millions of Israelites made it to the promised land. Only two trusted in God and obeyed Him fully. What a lesson.

So, there I was in full combat mode. I was back to wanting to protect my sister from her pastor. I did what I knew as a child. In order to protect and to fight, I became an uncontrollable lion. I knew my sister's weakness. I saw a con-artist taking advantage of her and knew what was to come. My instincts to protect her jumped in and for five years I fought with all my might to protect her against this man. For five years, I confronted my sister and told her what I thought about his teaching. Everything that he told her to do, I would come back and show her how he was wrong. I went in with my sword swinging, never considering that I might be taking the wrong approach. I never once approached my sister out of love. It was always out of frustration over what this man was doing to her. Not once did I ask God for wisdom on how to approach her. I reacted out of fear that he was going to take advantage of her. Symbolically I drew out my sword of the Spirit and started cutting out eyes. Matthew 5:29 says, **"If your right eye causes you to sin, gouge it out and throw it away. It is better for you to lose one part of your body than for your whole body to be thrown into hell."** And when that did not work, I would, symbolically, chop off a foot or two. **"If your hand or your foot causes you to sin, cut it off and throw it away. It is better for you to enter life maimed or crippled than to have two hands or two feet and be thrown into eternal fire. Then when that didn't work I would chop off a hand."** (Matthew 18:8) **"If your hand causes you to sin, cut it off. It is better for you to enter life maimed than with two hands to go into hell, wherever the fire never goes out."** (Mark 9:43).

Remember, I am the master justifier. I always seem to come up with a perfect reason to do the things I do. Scriptures can be taken way out of context without an intimate relationship with the Holy Spirit who guides us with the real meaning. I slowly began to realize that these scriptures had nothing to do with my sister's situation. My sister was already going to heaven. These pertain to unsaved people whose lifestyles are preventing them from receiving the salvation of Jesus. I recognized that it is up to the person themselves to cut off their own body part; however, I was not thinking like that at the time. This is what happens when fear leads us instead of allowing God's spirit to lead us.

For five solid years, I was completely frustrated and angry with my sister because she would not listen to me. I wondered why (sarcasm). After all, I was only trying to help her. But I was coming on way too strong and, in a sense, cutting her to pieces with my verbal sword. It is no wonder that she fled from my advice.

I can hardly believe that I used to be like that and be so outspoken. I recall saying to people, "I feel like a lion trapped in a cage." Now I see, I WAS trapped in a cage and good thing I was. I was so filled with anger that God had to trap me in order to protect the poor unexpected sheep out there. Can you imagine what I would have been like not locked up? Fortunately, I only attacked my one sister. I thought that my friend who confronted me about praying for the wrong request was bad. I made her look like Mary Poppins.

If you are anything like me, then you are not afraid to confront people. I simply will say whatever comes to my mind. I am not thinking that I am better than anyone; I just have a problem keeping my mouth closed when I see unrighteous behavior. I think that people like me have a harder time of letting go of this characteristic because it is exactly what enables us to be leaders. We are able to cut through the fog, pinpoint the issue, and address it straight on. The ability to lead is obviously not the problem. The problem is the tendency to want to control and to be too demanding in the process. But this is how God made me and why would I want to be anything other than who God made me?

One day I had this vision, meaning, it is like a dream but while awake. I was holding the world on my shoulders. Stacked on top of the world were tons of items, like houses, cars, buildings, etc. Then I heard the Lord say to me, "Cassia when are you going to let me help you? When are you going to cast all of your cares on me?" Then I heard God say to Jesus, "Watch this." God put a small chair on the top of this mountain of objects. I became a little weak in the knees, but I continued to hold everything up. I then heard them laughing at me in a loving sort of way as if they were saying, "Bless her heart. When will she learn?" God did create me to be how I am for a reason; however, if I refuse to learn how to lean on Him and if I think that I can do everything in my own strength, then God will have to remove my strength so that I can learn to trust in Him. He was teaching me how to lean on His strength instead.

I was approaching the situation with my sister with the completely wrong template. I did not look at this as a trial and a chance to grow and change into a better person. I never stopped to ask God what junk He was trying to empty out of me to make room for more of His goodness. I did not have any peace and was making every decision out of fear. I was so afraid that my sister was going to be taken advantage of which was exactly what happened. Her pastor took full advantage of her weaknesses and because I did not ask God for wisdom, I was unable to help her.

What I learned has been one of the greatest and most helpful revelations in my life. Making a decision out of fear simply does not work. A correct decision can only be made when one has inner peace. With that peace, comes the ability to love. With love, comes the ability to correct someone lovingly and they will then be more likely to receive that correction. This will not work every time;

however, chances are for a much higher success rate if a correction is made out of love.

    Jesus was always filled with love. Never did he correct someone out of fear or frustration. Even when he overturned the money collector's tables in the temple, it was because He saw the injustice towards the people who were being forced to pay for unnecessary items. Jesus corrected the Pharisees out of love for others and showed the Pharisees their errors. They chose not to listen and chose not turn from their wrong ways of thinking. It is our choices that set us apart.

    One day after years of battling with my sister, the Lord gave me a vision. The vision was so real, it was as if I were watching a movie. The vision showed my sister's destiny and the steps she needed to take in order to fulfill it. I was so excited about what the Lord showed me as it was an incredible plan. It was everything her heart desired. However, the Lord told me I could not tell her about it until she was in North Carolina. He said, "The people she was around would abort what He was birthing in her." I was confused by that statement, but I listened to the Lord and did not tell her until the Lord wanted me to. That did not stop me from telling every family member and friend I had about the vision because it was that amazing. I knew that no one would tell her.

    Several months later the Lord gave me a prophesy and told me that this same sister would lose her job. At first I was saddened by that, but the Lord continued to speak His word of prophesy. He told me not to worry because He was going to use her twin sister as a provision for her. This is what I love about God, He always has a plan for our lives. As long as we listen and obey, no circumstance will ever be to difficult to face. He then continued to speak telling me, "As a sign of what I was hearing was from Him, her twin sister would move." The most interesting thing was that I remembered how in previous months, the Lord revealed a vision for my older sister's destiny and God told me not to share the vision with her until she was in North Carolina. At that point in time, I did not understand what that meant. I thought, "share with her the vision when we get together in North Carolina for Christmas." Now, it was all becoming clear because her twin sister lives in North Carolina, and I should share the vision of her destiny when she acts upon the prophesy and moves to North Carolina.

The Lord did not reveal to me the timing of any of this, so I just wrote it all down and put it aside. Within three months, the twin of my oldest sister called me, and, unexpectedly, told me she had just put her house on the market. I was ecstatic to hear the news! I then began to share with her about the prophesy the Lord had told me months prior. She too was ecstatic! She loved the idea of having her twin sister live with her. She told me she would look for a house big enough for all of them to live with her for as long as they needed.

I had no doubt that the word the Lord gave me was from Him. I spoke to all of my family members to share the good news about what the Lord was doing for my older sister and shared with them how excited I was that I would soon be able to share with my older sister the wonderful vision God had planned for her destiny.

Three months after my sister moved, my older sister was laid off. It was just as the Lord had said. My whole family was so excited to see how God was going to use her hard situation for her good in the end. Everybody knew about my vision for her destiny and the prophecy and could clearly see it all coming together. We all knew my older sister would listen as the pieces were coming together so perfectly it would be hard to deny the truth of my words.

The Bible says that you will know if a vision or prophesy is from God if it comes to pass. I saw my older sister move two times within an eleven month time period with the prompting of her pastor, so I was sure she would move when the instruction was coming from the Lord.

When my sister was given notice that she had been laid off, I decided to call her at work and tell her about what the prophesy, not the vision, the Lord said. I was excited to share with her, but also scared to tell her. We had had several intense years of bickering and the fear set in. I did not want to tell her because I was afraid that, like before, she would not listen. By that time, I had learned the importance of approaching people lovingly and only hoped this would make the difference. I still was nervous though. I decided to have my mother and other sister on the phone with me when I called her. I thought maybe they could make sure I was sharing what I believed with her in the best possible way. I so desperately wanted her to receive all that God had to give her. I did not want any of my past mistakes to prevent her from hearing and obeying God. I was willing to do whatever I needed to help her make the right choice.

Unfortunately, when I told her the prophecy about losing her job, her twin sister moving, and how it all came to pass, she chose not to listen. She told me I was trying to control her. It absolutely broke my heart. I was devastated. It has been two and a half years since this all happened and she is still living here in New England. Even though everything was beautifully laid out for her, she has never been able to hear the incredible vision about her dynamic destiny. For a long time, I felt sad for her. I know that the vision God gave me for her lines up perfectly with her true heart's desire. Her entire life she has spoken about wanting to do the things the Lord showed me He would make possible for her to do.

I still hold onto the vision tightly. I constantly pray about it and believe that one day my sister will walk in her destiny. I will continue to pray and believe.

It was not until recently that the Lord revealed something eye-opening to me about this situation. I felt overwhelmed with sadness for her thinking that she had missed her calling and the Lord dropped this on me saying, "I never told you when she was supposed to move. I just said she was going to move and as a sign her twin sister would move."

Wow! What a revelation! I could not believe what I was hearing. How could I have been so blind? This is why knowing God's timing is even more crucial than ever. My sister was right. I was being controlling at the time. I was trying to get her to move right away. His timing for her could be at any time. It is not up to me to know when.

What I love about God is that He is always in control, even if I cannot see it at the time. We have to remember that. We have to know that He loves us and He wants us to succeed.

Now, I have new hope for her. I truly believe that God's timing is somehow connected to our readiness and willingness to obey His will. I do not believe that it should be taking my sister this long to listen, but God knows best. I know that He is patient and He waits for us to be ready. I no longer feel sadness for my sister. I believe that God will do for her exactly what he has promised. My faith has grown stronger with each step through this experience.

As with all my trials, I am left asking myself, "What else have I missed? What else are you trying to teach me during this hardship?" I thank God for being faithful, patient, and loving. I am grateful that He offers us a personal relationship that includes loving instruction and correction when we make mistakes.

I clearly see how these last two and a half years of sadness have purpose. I see how every prayer I prayed for her destiny was heard by God. John 1:1 states, **"In the beginning was the Word, and the Word was with God, and the Word was God."** It was by words that all of creation was made. It is our words that are in alignment with God's will that are spoken out of our mouths that also can create. I see now, how He has used my pain as inspiration to stay determined in believing she will reach her destiny.

I cannot believe I never thought to ask God, "When?" However, I am grateful that, **"God uses all bad for good to those who love Him and are called according to His purpose."** (Romans 8:28). I just assumed that when she was laid off, she would move right away to North Carolina. Learn from my mistake. Ask God what His timing is for every situation.

As I think of all of those years I tried to help my older sister, I keep thinking about Paul. I think of him when he was Saul. He loved God with all of his heart. He was one of the top ranked Pharisees. He knew the Mosaic scriptures inside and out. His heart was right. I think that was why God chose him. Saul thought that he was doing the right thing by adamantly disputing the claims of Christians. He believed they opposed God's laws and had to fight and protect against such heresy.

I hate to admit that I acted very much like him. Something happens to a person like me who is a natural fighter; one who naturally wants to protect people. My sword starts swinging before I even look around the room to see whom I might accidentally hurt. What I love about Saul's story is how all it took was one time of hearing

God's voice and he instantly converted. He went from killing Christians to guiding Christians after just one Godly encounter. He chose to get rid of his old template and chose to allow God to give him a new template. He allowed God to change him from the inside out. Obviously I was not there yet. I was still out killing Christians or whoever happened to be in my way when I started swinging my sword. Like Saul, I also saw that my actions were incorrect and decided to allow God to change me and my ways of thinking in order for Him to be able to use me. I needed a new name too.

My sister continued to let this pastor control her life. I made it all too easy for the pastor as I sent my sister running for her life. It was not until my other sister called me, the one with the kidney disease who was waiting for a transplant, and said that she could not take it anymore that I was able to redirect my focus. She wanted to end her life. I reacted strongly and kicked into an entirely new level of protection (if that was even possible). Picture a lion locked in a cage with a herd of antelopes standing right in front of him. I was foaming at the mouth. Even though, I just went through this five-year-long battle with my other sister, I still had not fully let go of my old template.

I called my two other sisters, including the one I had been battling with, and did a three way call to tell them about my ill sister's comments. One sister was like me; she went into protection mode. We started developing a plan. We were going to take turns going to her house and helping her out. She obviously needed family around her in this hard time. One sister disagreed, believing that we were overreacting in our fear. She encouraged us all to overcome our fear and help our troubled sister with prayer alone.

Was she right? Was I afraid? Of course. I just heard my suffering sister say she wanted to die. I live hundreds of miles away from her. I was unsure of what she would do. Did I need to trust God? Of course. Did I need to pray for her? Of course. However, sometimes people need more than just to hear you say, "I'll be praying for you." Sometimes we need to be the answer to their prayers.

It was clearly time for me to drop the issues with my older sister and direct my energy and attention towards my sister with the kidney disease. She needed me more than ever and I needed to separate myself from what was causing me to be angry in order to be more helpful to the sister who was struggling

God knew I needed to be a lamb and not a lion. I saw how my tactics were not working with my older sister. I had to change my way of thinking. I had to change my strategy in how I approached people. I knew that if I did not change, my sister could die. I knew that in order to hear from God, He had to totally transform me into a lamb.

I have learned that with God, we can never fail. He will just keep repeating the trials until we learn. Because I am strong and stubborn, He needs to make them even harder. God knows our breaking point. He knows just how much we can take without destroying us in order to help us. For me, it took seven years of battling one sister and waiting on another sister to have a kidney transplant before I could see that my war tactics were not working. We have to be able to see that these trials have a purpose. It is not God punishing us; it is His way of communicating with us and teaching us how to be more like Himself. And equipping us to have what we need to fulfill our destinies.

The good thing is that I am persistent. I am determined to finish my race. However, that is the bad thing about me too. I will spend all my energy pushing down a door that God has shut for a reason. Sometimes I do not realize it is God at work so I bring out the ax. If that does not work, I bring out the dynamite. I do whatever it takes to get that door open.

I think that is why God started showing me the importance of fruit. If God is in the plan, there will be that fruit we talked about in earlier chapters. If the fruits of the spirit are not present whatsoever, then I have learned to stop and re-evaluate the situation. Sometimes, the best thing to do is to walk away. If we do not have a clear direction, we need to wait. We cannot just start doing things in our own method. We should not start kicking down doors that God has closed. We should not pick up our sword and start swinging when there are innocent people in the room.

I did not have the peace back then that I have now. I was not trusting God. I always thought that I had to make things happen. I had to take all of my natural abilities and strengths and help the people that needed help. Obviously I was wrong. Everything I did backfired with my older sister. Instead of helping her; I pushed her away. Instead of showing her I was there to love and protect her, which I was, she misinterpreted my actions to mean I wanted to control her. That is exactly what happens when we try to correct people without love and instead, out of frustration and fear.

Every decision we make needs to come from a place of peace. If we do not have peace, we are unable to react to a situation the way God wants us to. Granted, we could be in a new season of our lives in Christ or discordant with God's timing, but try to zero in on that peace that the Bible says, "passes all understanding" and it will help greatly to keep focused and balanced when we face difficult situations. Remember, God is working with us as His spokesman and His hands and feet, trying always to bless us with faith, hope, and love no matter what is going on around us.

Chapter 8
Timing Is Everything

The Lord gave me another vision one day while I was living with my aunt in South Carolina. In this vision, I saw a yellow, two-story house with a white porch. In the back was a walkout basement. The Lord then said, "This is your personal training studio." That was an odd vision to me considering I was not a personal trainer. You can imagine my surprise! Being the person that I am, I started driving around the neighborhoods with my brother looking for a house that fit that description. This is the kind of faith I have. I did not own a car or a training certificate, but I had a vision that I believed was from the Lord.

I continued to search for the house for a couple of months, then the Lord had to say to me, "Cassia, don't you think you should become a trainer first then start your business?" Remember, timing.

I walked into a local fitness center, without any experience and asked, "Would you hire me as a trainer?" Surprisingly, they said, "Yes," and I started working there. They helped me to get certified. Then at the age of twenty-three I stepped out in faith, like I always did, and bought a car. I was so excited! For the first time in my whole life, I did not have to depend on anyone else to get me to where I needed to go. I was so happy and grateful for God's provision.

I continued to work at the fitness center and when I became a certified trainer, I thought I was ready to open up my own gym. I am certified. I have a car. I am ready to go! Nope. The Lord told me to move back up to Connecticut and personal train there. I made one phone call from South Carolina to a gym in Connecticut, where my sister lived, and asked for a job. They agreed to hire me so I moved back in with my sister and became a personal trainer at this gym. After working there six months, I started to dislike the owner of the gym and I wanted to quit. "I did not have to take this because I had a vision," was my puffed up thinking. In response to prayer, I believe the Lord told me I had to continue working there for another 6 months. I gritted my teeth and continued to work. Good lion.

One year had now passed. I could not wait to leave this company. I told my boyfriend at the time that it was time for me to open my gym. He went online and started looking for places for rent. We saw one place and I thought it was perfect. I had totally forgotten about the vision I had two years earlier. I told the Landlord that I liked the space. The next step was to look for gym equipment. During that process, we realized we were not going to be able to get fitness equipment into the space we had seen. It was located on a second floor with no elevator. When I expressed my concern to the property owner, he told me that if I could wait just one month, he had a spot on the bottom floor that would be opening up. I agreed and continued ordering equipment.

The equipment showed up at the new location and as I began to move it into the building, the Lord reminded me of my vision. The building I was moving into was a yellow, two-story building with a white porch and I was in the walkout basement. It was unreal! The timing could not have been more perfect. God knew exactly when this location would be ready. If I had pushed for my own way, I could possibly have ruined God's plan for me. Not only that, but because I stayed at the gym for a year, I had five clients that loved me and said that they would go wherever I went to be able to keep me as their personal trainer. Before I even opened my doors, my bills were paid. These five clients stayed with me three times a week for the entire four years I was open. In addition, the first week the gym was opened, five more clients showed up and stayed with me three times a week for four years. I cannot stress enough the importance of timing.

    Life is full of seasons. Even when we have direct guidance from God in our lives, we still have to be sensitive to the smaller nuances. We also have to be sensitive to the fact that God may close a door just as quickly as He opens one. For example, when the Lord led me to open my gym, from the way it all came together, it was obvious to me that it was His will for me. However, it did not mean that I was supposed to stay there forever. For me, it was a four-year long season.

    How will you know when it is time to move on and God is closing the door? This is where the importance of fruit comes into play. We always need to take a step back in our lives and see if the outcome of our thoughts and actions are producing the fruit I mention periodically. We should constantly be re-evaluating our lives. We need to always look for the evidence that God's hand is on our situation.

    For me, I knew my time as a fitness center owner was coming to an end when I started to lose my peace. Galatians 5:22-23 reads, **"But the fruit of the Spirit is**

love, joy, peace, forbearance, kindness, goodness, faithfulness, gentleness and self-control. Against such things there is no law." When I first opened up my gym, I woke up every day saying, "Thank you, Jesus, for my gym." I could not wait to get to work each day. I would invest everything that I had into my clients in order to help them achieve their goals. Suddenly one day, I did not feel like going. I started showing up five minutes late. Then it started to feel like a heavy burden. I did not understand what was going on so I prayed asking God for better understanding.

"God, why don't I like my gym anymore? What is wrong with me? Do I have sin in my life? Am I allowing Satan to negatively affect me somehow?" were the gist of my prayers.

He told me, "No, it is none of that. I want you to sell your gym and help your sister with her music career."

"What? I asked. That is crazy. You gave me this gym. You gave me the vision."

"Yes, but now it is time for a new season and, yes, I gave you that gym, so I can take it away. That is why your heart is not in it any more. It is time to let go." It is so important to keep your identity in Christ and not in what your job is. I am not a personal trainer. I am not a waitress. I am not a day care worker. I am not a writer. I am an ambassador to Christ. I am who He has called me to be in that particular season.

It was the hardest thing because I had grown so close to the women that came to my gym. We all went through a lot together. I knew they would be upset, but I had to obey God.

I told all of the women I was closing the gym. They were sad, of course, but happy for me in whatever I was going to pursue. One of my clients told me that she knew a woman who wanted to open up a gym like mine. I called her to come look at the equipment. She bought all of the equipment down to the clock on the wall. It was amazing. Again, timing is everything and being connected to the Father of Time is always a bonus. If I had waited one more month, the woman who bought all of my equipment could have purchased equipment elsewhere.

I cannot say it often enough: we HAVE to be in God's timing. We have to look every day for God's evidence in whatever situation we are in. The moment the fruit begins to fade, ask God what He is doing.

God used this whole experience to teach me how to discern the difference between Satan's trickery getting in my way or God closing the door. I was slowly learning not to use an axe or dynamite to open the doors God has closed. The way everything came to pass was so perfect and so peaceful and this is how I knew I was right where God wanted me.

As a twist, when I received the check from the woman who bought all of my equipment, the Lord told me to give every dollar towards my sister's music and so, I did.

Chapter 9
Letting Go Of Natural Abilities

One of the most important lessons I learned came out of one of the hardest trials I went through. God had to actually prep me for this one. There was a period of time that lasted about a year and a half before my sister had her kidney transplant. God used this time as a training ground to get me ready for what was coming next. Of course, I did not realize it until I was already in it, but once involved, there was no turning back. Unfortunately, I had the wrong way of thinking again and this caused some problems.

For the next year and a half, God stripped away who I knew myself to be. I thought I would go down to my sister's house and that God, combined with my faith, would heal her. I intended to visit my sister and use my natural strength and planning abilities to run her household and fix everything. I was going to be my usual lion self. That is not at all what happened. In fact, for 18 months, while flying back and forth from Connecticut to North Carolina, I proceeded to lose every bit of strength I had. First, I lost faith in myself. I cannot tell you how many times I prayed for my sister. I laid my hands on her. I told her all the things she needed to do in order to receive God's healing. Nothing worked. Where was the telltale fruit?

Because of the hectic flying schedule, I was unable to exercise as I was accustomed to and I began to lose all my physical strength. I was always very strong. I competed in Fitness America Pageants. So when my muscular strength faded, I felt as if I were another person. My courage, my faith, my trust in God, my direction, my plans, and my goals all began to wane. I felt lost. I had no idea what I was going to do and how I was going to do it. All I knew was that my sister needed me and I had to be there for her.

I already knew how to be a lion. That came naturally. Of course, it is easier to do what one knows. God clearly made me a lion for a reason. I know that I would not have survived childhood if I had not had the strength, faith, and courage that I had been given. My natural gifts had kept me on the straight and narrow path in life thus far and I was also able to lead in the right direction from a very young age. God had used my history to teach me about the benefit of being a lion and I have always been grateful for my natural leadership skills.

I was in a whole new season now. Life is a series of seasons, I believe, and we need to be sensitive to God's timing. We need to keep looking for fruit as an indicator of whether it is time to move on to another. Clearly, I was out of season. My dear sister did not need a lion; she needed a lamb.

God always searches for those He can work along side with. Prior to my sister's operation, I continually cried out to God saying, "Use me, Lord. Use me." We tend to think we know how He will guide us. I felt certain He wanted me to conduct some spiritual warfare. "I'll fight some demons. I love showing those demons who is boss, I will pray and pray until my sister is healed," I thought. God had a different plan and I am glad He did!

It was not until recently, looking back at my time in North Carolina that I could see God's purpose clearly. Imagine this scenario: My sister was lying in bed exhausted just trying to survive. Dinner needed to be made. Homework needed to be completed. Baths needed to be given. If I had been feeling like my regular self back then, I would have been in her living room praying at the top of my lungs and shouting at the devil to leave her alone. I think I would have pushed her over the edge had God not weakened me as well. My sister did not need me to be a warrior; she needed me to be something I was not, a tender lamb.

The best thing about being forced beyond our natural abilities is that we arrive at a point where we need to depend on God completely. Not only does God want to develop our natural talents, He also wants to give us supernatural talents - talents that come directly from Him. By the grace of God, I was able to soften and become the gentle person that my sister needed most at that time in her life. To accomplish that, I had to totally trust and rely upon God.

God is always trying to remind us that even though He gave us our natural abilities, He wants to give us more than just what comes naturally. He wants to supply us with what we do not yet have. That way we can truly be all things to all people and better help others in their search for truth. In order to be that kind of person, we need to accept help from God.

As a lion, I was fearless, courageous, strong, determined, and a warrior. All of that is great and a true gift from God who made me; however, God wanted to give me more. Not only did He attempt to train the wild beast that I was, He also began working in my life to develop qualities that a lion clearly lacks: compassion, love, humility, gentleness, and kindness. Of course there were many times when I would demonstrate compassion, when I would see a person hurting or desperate and I would want to help. However, God wanted more. He wanted me to be able to love the unlovable at all times and be willing to give even to those who I felt did not deserve it. In order to receive that ability from God, I had to let go of my preconceived notions and allow Him to change my mind and heart.

Eventually, I began to recognize the purpose of each and every one of my trials. I never truly undstood why God was doing what He was doing. We might not ever truly have full understanding of what God is doing. Look at what happened to Adam and Eve when they took a bite of fruit from the Tree of Knowlege. However, I did start to see that each trial did have a purspose. Every single one was meant to help me let go of my wrong ways of thinking, to learn how to think the way God was thinking, as a tool for building a strong foundation for my destiny, or to help me have the mind of Christ. I Corinthinas 2:11-16 states, **"For who knows a person's thoughts except their own spirit within them? In the same way no one knows the thoughts of God ecxept the Spirit of God. 12 What we have received is not the spirit of the world, but the Spirit who is from God, so that we may understand what God has freely given us. 13 This is what we speak, not in words taught us by human wisdom but in words taught by the Spirit, explaining spiritual realities with Spirit-taught words. 14 The person without the Spirit does not accept the things that come from the Spirit of God but considers them foolishness, and cannot understand them because they are discerned only through the Spirit. 15 The person with the Spirit makes**

judgments about all things, but such a person is not subject to merely human judgment, for 16 "Who has known the mind of the Lord so as to instruct him?" But we have the mind of Christ. That is why trials are so difficult. We have to learn how to be taught by the Holy Spirit, not by the spirit of the world. Difficult experiences force us to face our insecurities and ask some big questions. What are you trying to teach me, God? What quality of yours are you trying to give to me? What about myself is blocking me from receiving more of your wisdom?

At times, we need to experience a place of weakness before we are willing to accept the changes God wants to help us make. Rest assured, for some of us, He is not getting rid of our natural abilities forever, just for a time as we learn to be totally dependent upon Him. Once we learn how to be totally dependent upon God and are walking in His abilities; then and only then can we be allowed to use our natural abilities to the fullest capacity. If God thinks that your natural abilities might be a deterrent for you, then and only then, would He not give them back. In my case, God created me with lion-like characteristics. Before He could let this lion out of its cage, He had to make sure I would not devour the lambs in my sheer desire to help them.

One day, God gave me another vision. I was looking through the eyes of a lion. In fact, I was the lion. I saw in the far distance a wolf. The wolf was standing out in the middle of an open green field. Beyond the wolf was a forest. As the lion, I knew I had to get to the wolf before he got to the forest. I knew instinctively it was my duty to capture this wolf and like a fearless lion, I charged after the wolf. I could hear myself breathing heavily. I could feel my paws digging deeply into the ground as I used my muscular legs to push faster and faster in order to gain speed. With every charge, I got closer and closer. I could see the wolf was almost to the forest tree line. Just as I thought the wolf was going to get away, I felt myself, press off my hind legs and leap into the air. As I landed, I grabbed the wolf by the neck with my sharp, strong teeth. Instantly, I felt a deep sense of pride. I sat on my hind legs with the prize wolf in my mouth, knowing I had done my job well.

Before long, however, the feeling of pride turned into a feeling of sadness. I heard God's voice say, "Turn around." Slowly I turned around. That is when my jaw dropped. The dead wolf fell out of my mouth and an overwhelming sense of sadness fell over me. As I looked out upon the open field I had run across in order to capture the wolf, I saw hundreds and hundreds of sheep. Each one was bloodied and injured in some way. I could hear them crying out in pain. I could see fear in their sweet little eyes. That is when the Lord said, "Cassia, you were so focused on getting the wolf that you did not see all of the sheep that were grazing in the field. You became so focused on capturing the enemy that you did not stop to ask me for a strategy. Yes, it is great that you captured the wolf; however, it does no good to me if you injure my sheep in the process. Satan knows your weaknesses. It means nothing to him to sacrifice one of his in order to destroy hundreds of mine." After that vision, I understood fully that I had to lay all of my abilities down in order for God to train me. I was accustomed to doing things in my own strength. I was a confident person who cared little about what people thought of me which made it particularly difficult to let go of my natural responses and let God lead me with the correct responses.

I will tell you a story as an example of how I was able to easily succeed in my own strength and abilities. As

I mentioned before, I love to dance. Everyone who knows me, knows this. One day a friend of mine came up to me and told me that there were auditions being held for hip-hop dancers. I always loved to dance hip-hop and was excited to attend the audition.

    I showed up to the audition. It was in a huge auditorium with a full audience, but that did not faze me at all. I noticed when I got there people were singing on the stage. I asked the person in charge about it. She told me that anyone wanting to audition for a dance part also had to do a singing audition. "I'm not a singer," I said. She told me if I did not sing, I could not dance. So I said I would sing.

    They called my name up to audition for the singing part. The piano player asked me what song I was going to sing. When I told him I did not have a song selected, he suggested I sing, "Happy Birthday," to which I agreed. Loudly and fearlessly, I sang the song from start to finish.

    Then they put us in groups of ten to learn the dance routine for the audition. They took the first group back stage and taught them the routine. While they went up on stage to audition, my group went back stage to learn the routine. Upon learning the routine, I realized it was nothing like hip-hop. I was a little confused, but I continued to learn the routine. Then they told us it was our turn to audition. As we were being lead out to the stage for the audition, I noticed people putting on tap shoes. That was when it hit me. This was not an audition for a hip-hop show at all, but was a musical including tap dancing. There I was on this stage doing a tap routine without tap shoes. I performed with confidence. That was all I knew to do although I had never taken a tap lesson in my life. I could not believe all I did that day.

The funniest thing about it was that I got a call back the next day to be in the chorus and to return for a second dance audition. They even told me to wear the same outfit never having noticed I was not wearing tap shoes. My point in telling this story is that I am always able to successfully accomplish what seems impossible to some. However, I was not even slightly interested in being in a musical. What good did it do me to have all of this confidence, if it was not what I wanted or what God wanted for me? The experience helped me realize that I would rather have my natural abilities developed by God, than have my own natural abilities carry me to success in things that I care little about. I was really, truly ready to let my natural abilities die, so that I could receive God's abilities into my life.

Chapter 10
Becoming Weak To Help The Weak

As a freshman in college, I got along with my roommate very well. Our college was in North Carolina, but she happened to be from Florida too and she owned a car. We traveled back and forth together between college and home during our school vacations.

At the time, I had a boyfriend who lived near my home in Florida who I had been dating since high school. When I went home for college breaks, I would spend time with him. I hung pictures of him on my dorm room wall and would talk about him with my roommate.

When we went home for Thanksgiving break, my boyfriend's mother offered to drop me off at my roommates house on our way back up to college so that my boyfriend could meet my roommate. We were both excited that she was going to meet him. However, my excitement ended abruptly. During the time I was home, my boyfriend broke up with me. At first, I was devastated. I cried for two days, but by the day it was time to return to college, I had fully recovered and was ready to move on.

When I showed up at my roommate's house and my boyfriend was not there, she of course wondered why. I told her that he had broken up with me. She was so sad. I assured her I was fine.

When we got back up to the dorm, I took down all of the pictures and threw them away. I was over him and ready to move on and focus on school. My roommate, however, was not able to get over it as easily. She kept asking me if I was all right and I assured her that I was fine.

That is when something strange started happening. I noticed that she did not want to spend time with me as much and she chose to be with other friends. It got to the point that we stopped talking to each other. The silence was just too unbearable. Eventually I moved out and got my own room.

Several months later, I saw her in a hallway and asked her if I had ever done anything to offend her. She shared with me that when she saw how strong I was about the break up, it made her feel weak. She was used to being the strong one in her relationships and felt intimidated by me. I was shocked at what she was saying, as nobody had ever said that to me before. I could not ever have imagined that could happen. How could one's natural abilities actually cause someone harm? Remember the scripture about having to become weak in order to relate to the weak?

The next year, I transferred schools and had another roommate. Just as with the first one, things started out great. We had a lot of fun together and got along well. Shortly into the semester, I noticed that she was taking over our entire dorm and it started to become clear to me that she was a very controlling person. When living in these tiny little dorms, respect for each other's space is mandatory.

As always, I confronted the situation. I told her she needed to keep her belongings on her side of the room. I do not know if she had ever had anyone confront her in that way, but she did not like it. Our relationship became progressively worse. I remember calling my grandmother, because I could not locate my mother, crying and asking her to pray for me. I never thought to look at this as a trial God was using to try to teach me something so I moved out and, just like before, and got my own room.

Each time I lived in solitary, I absolutely loved it. Growing up, I had to share a room with my three sisters until I was fourteen years old, so living alone was a treat. I enjoyed the opportunity to read and pray in solitude. When everyone else was out socializing, I was in my room or sitting out under a tree reading and talking to God. I would tell Jesus all the time how I did not need anybody. I felt that all I needed was Him.

One day I was in my usual prayer routine, thinking about my second roommate and thinking about how refreshing it was to not need anybody when the Lord said to me, "Cassia, did you ever think that they might need you? Did you ever think that I put you with those roommates on purpose? I wanted you to give something to them and I was going to give to you what you needed in order to do so." That was when I started to realize that being overly confident in myself, and proclaiming that I did not need anyone else was not a healthy attitude. What good is being a Christian if you just stay locked up in a room by yourself? The hardest thing is to get out there and try to be around people that drive you crazy. It was easy for me to be confident and have peace if I kept myself secluded, but as soon as troubles came, I fled.

The Lord also revealed to me that the template that I had created in my mind needed revision. All of those years of watching my mother gather us up and leave the house when my dad was having an episode, taught me to run away from any circumstance that felt difficult. Understandably, she had to take her children out of harm's way. However, it was not leaving the house to avoid my father's violence that was the problem; it was my mother's silence on the event after we returned that was most disturbing to me. Never once did I witness her confronting my father regarding his behavior. When we would return to our home, my father would be watching television or have fallen asleep and my mother would let the sleeping dog lie. My father was never held accountable for his actions. Year after year, time after time, I would watch her avoid confrontation at all cost. It was not until the Lord revealed to me the similarity between my mother's coping mechanisms and my own that I began to change. Moving out of my dorm was running away from the trials God had put before me.

Naturally, it is easiest to be alone; however, God did not want me to be alone. In my sophomore year, I finally had a roommate I got along with well and we remained roommates. She had a boyfriend though whom she was always with and I started to feel very lonely. While other classmates enjoyed attending football games, basketball games, or shopping with friends, I was in my dorm room or outside praying.

During one of my times with God, I asked Him why I was feeling so alone and sad. He reminded me of a girl I noticed back in high school. One day while I was waiting outside with the rest of my class for the bell to ring, I noticed a girl with a cleft pallet. I remember feeling sadness for her that she had to live with this defect and wanted very badly to help her fix it, but realized that there was nothing I could do for her. Whenever I would see her at school, I would feel such empathy for her.

On that day that I was asking God about my loneliness, He revealed to me that the girl with the cleft pallet was feeling the same way. I began crying buckets of tears for I realized that I could have provided the "fix" for the girl with the deformity for what this girl needed was, not an operation, but a friend to help her feel loved and not alone.

I believe the pain I felt in those moments of crying was the Lord softening me in order to be able to relate better with people. He was again causing me to feel weak and humble in order to help the weak. That is why it is so important not to rely on our own natural abilities. How empowering it is to operate in God's abilities instead of merely our own and to see situations through His eyes! Think about Jesus. He was loving and compassionate, but he also had great authority given to him by his father. When he would walk up to a person who was possessed, he would speak with authority like a lion and cast that demon out. But with the Samaritan woman who was caught in the act of adultery and about to be stoned to death, Jesus knew she did not need the judgment of a lion, but the grace and gentleness of a lamb. Did Jesus correct her? Of course. However, He did so with such grace, forgiveness, and mercy that it spoke to her through and through and her heart and life were changed.

The whole purpose of this book is to demonstrate how to look at our trials in the way that God intended them to be viewed. In other words, to see each situation we find ourselves in through His eyes. He is teaching us all to approach Him with this attitude: "God I already know my natural abilities, what are the additional abilities you are want to give me to equip me to get through this?"

All of the trials I have mentioned throughout this book have led me to this one point in time. I am so definitely a lion and God cannot release me until He can trust that I will not devour His lambs. Everything that has happened to me over my thirty six years on this earth is all about me letting go of my natural abilities in in order to allow God to develop them. And to learn how to receive God's abilities.

For years I have begged God to make me able to love the unlovable and to want to give to those who do not deserve it. God will never allow us to fail. He will keep bringing opportunities into our lives that will allow our prayers to be answered if they are prayers that line up with His will. When we finally decide to obey God and do what He asks of us, we should be ready to do this at all cost.

Chapter 11
The Lamb Has Emerged

As I mentioned previously, one of my sisters was born with a kidney disease. None of us knew about it until she was twenty five. Giving birth to her daughter some years later triggered a bodily response and the severity of her disease became more evident. Within four years after the birth of her daughter, her kidneys were functioning at only 35 percent capacity. She was going to need help with everyday functions.

My journeys between Connecticut and North Carolina began. At first, I would fly down occasionally and stay for a couple of weeks at a time to try to lighten the load. In my usual lion mode, I used my strength and energy to do whatever needed to be done - laundry, dishes, grocery shopping, childcare, anything. I relied upon my faith to pray for her believing that God was going to heal her miraculously. I became a warrior for her fighting against the evil forces that can cause sickness and pain. I quoted every scripture out loud that I could think of during my prayer times. "No weapon formed against her will prosper," is an example. I felt it was my responsibility to straighten everything out and to call in the healing forces.

I started to analyze the situation to figure out what everyone's emotional needs were and tried to meet their needs. If I felt something was wrong, I would confront the problem hoping to make the necessary corrections. Even after years of trails and years when God was teaching me to lean on Him, I still had not learned to rely on His strength. I should have learned to ask God what He might be trying to teach me. Instead, for the next two years, I continued to rely upon my own strength.

One day, while home in Connecticut, I received the phone call that I had been dreading. My sister called to report that she was scheduled for a kidney transplant in one month. At that point, her kidney function was down to a mere 8 percent. Somehow, I was still shocked by the news. I realized there was absolutely nothing I could do on my own to change her medical situation. She would have to have both kidneys taken out and replaced with one functional one, which meant she would to be out of commission for the next four months. With a six year old and a two year old, she would definitely need help. However, I knew I could not live there for the next four months with the same attitude I was accustomed to having. I realized I would have to change if I wanted things to go well.

God started dealing strongly with me making it clear that I needed to put down my spiritual sword. I could not be a lion in this situation. I argued with God, telling him it was difficult to be other than who He created me to be. I believed He wanted me to demonstrate qualities that I did not feel I had and I realized that the only possible way for that to happen was to obey Him and put down my sword. God was so intent on what He wanted that He actually sent strangers into my life to tell me, "God told me to tell you to put down your sword." I was frightened to get involved at the level I knew was going to be necessary and felt unsure of myself knowing that I was not allowed to use any of my natural abilities. I had to totally trust and lean on God and I had no idea what that was going to be like.

Before traveling to North Carolina for an extended stay, I felt God telling me not only that I needed to put down my sword, but also that He was going to fill me with compassion. I understood that in order for God to fill me with compassion, I had to make a little extra room. Letting go of my inner warrior was what God was requiring of me. I knew what God was trying to do and that made me feel very anxious. I asked God, "What if I am not able to keep my sword down? Will you still make it possible for me to help her?" I was afraid that I would still tend to be confrontational with any disagreement and just had to trust that if I stayed focused on God, I could handle the impending situations appropriately.

Now the battle began. I arrived in North Carolina at my sister's home. I felt like I had walked into a World War II triage camp. The children were wounded. My sister was wounded. Her husband was wounded. They had all experienced something traumatic. I felt like I needed to get in there and bandage their wounds. But immediately, God instructed me to keep my sword down, to do everyday functions, and to deal with the facts, not the emotions.

At first it was working well and I was able to just focus on the tasks at hand. Then it became more difficult. God never promised it was going to be easy. He just said, "Do what I ask. Obey, trust, and lean on me." The struggle started small. My sister told me how to do her laundry. She wanted to make sure I hung up certain clothes so they would not shrink. Fine. Then, while I was cooking, she would come over and turn on the light over the stove saying that was what she did to remind her the oven is on.

Fine too. Then she instructed me to turn off the radio, air conditioner, and DVD player in the car before I turned the car off. Next, she began leaving sticky notes filled with detailed instructions on all kinds of chores and that really started to get on my nerves.

Normally, I would have had no problem telling her, "Hey, I am here at my own will doing the best I can for you so leave me alone." But the Lord told me to put my sword down and so I did. I knew I had to obey Him if I was going to be able to get through this ordeal, so I held my tongue. Whenever I started to boil over, I would turn on some Christian music and start singing and dancing and focusing on Jesus instead of my problems. It worked for about two months then I almost had a break down. I hit the point when I needed some relief from the everyday tasks and asked my sister's husband if it was okay if I hire the nanny for one extra day. He, of course, agreed and said I could hire her for as many days as I needed. I asked the nanny to come an extra day, but when my sister found out about it, she lashed out at me yelling, "It's my money. How dare you call and have her come another day! If you needed help, you should have let me know and I would have called someone else who would come and worked for free!" She ranted about not spending her money. It took all the strength I had to respond with kindness. My sister cancelled the nanny for that day.

The next day when the kids were in school and she was at a medical appointment, I sat in her living room and cried out to God saying, "God, you said if I obeyed you and put down my sword, you would give me compassion. I need that compassion right now for my sister if I am going to be able to stay here for another two months." Immediately, I saw myself lying on a boat with Jesus. I saw a storm all around me. Just like the scriptures in Mark

4:37-39, "**A furious squall came up, and the waves broke over the boat, so that it was nearly swamped. Jesus was in the stern, sleeping on a cushion. The disciples woke him and said to him, "Teacher, don't you care if we drown?"** He got up, rebuked the wind and said to the waves, "Quiet! Be still! Then the wind died down and it was completely calm."

That was the vision I saw except I was on the boat, not the disciples. Unlike the disciples, I was not afraid. A sense of peace came over me like never before and in that moment, I understood what it felt like to have peace, like Jesus did, during a storm. Then, I began to feel every emotion my sister was feeling. I saw her situation from her perspective and felt all her fears and doubts. I realized she was asking herself some big questions like, "What would it be like if I died? What is going to happen to my children? Who will raise them? How sad would they be without me?" I started to understand that she had no control over whether she would live or die and was, understandably, immersed in fear.

The insight gave me complete compassion for my sister. I understood that she was feeling completely out of control. She was not able to take care of her children and was having to rely on others to do everything for her. As she barked out her orders, she was only trying to get me do what she would have wanted to do for her family and she was simply very scared. Finally, I had the compassion and peace I needed to get through the entire ordeal...or so I thought.

A week went by after this amazing break through and everything was progressing smoothly. I believed the next two months would be a breeze. I thought, "Yes! I know how to have peace during a storm." Again, my faith was going to be tested.

It was the week my sister was having her transplant. Her husband was the donor and for a week, they were both going to be in the hospital. Because both of them were going to be gone and the children were so young, I asked my mother to come and stay with me to help care for the children. She was more than happy to come and help. Once she arrived, everything was going well. There was the expected amount of emotion and stress for everyone in the house. Within a few days though, my mother was not dealing well with the situation.

The surgeries went well. My brother-in-law was going to be able to come back home. The night before he was to come home, I awoke in the middle of the night by strange noises in the house. I got up to see what was going on and discovered my mother in the kitchen talking to herself and pacing. I asked her what was wrong and she began to mumble about how she could not be in the house with my brother-in-law. I asked her to sit down so we could talk. I allowed my mother to speak her mind. As she spoke, I silently prayed. I knew that just a week earlier, God had given me a major breakthrough and knew He could do the same for her. As I prayed, the Lord began to speak through me. He started saying to my mother, "Just focus on the children. Don't think about anyone or anything else. I will give you what you need." I was so filled with love and compassion for my mother just then. I was crying and said to her, "Mom, just agree with me on this. God will help you." And then, my mother said something to me that I will never forget. She laughed at me and said in a harsh tone, "Agreement? I will never agree with you."

I honestly felt sick to my stomach. Here we were, sharing a traumatic family event. We needed to support one another, and she laughed at me. I got up, walked away and cried like I had never cried before. It was more like wailing and it continued for a few hours. When I finally stopped crying, Jesus said, "I had to let her go and I was in mourning of the loss of the relationship with my mother." My mother was always someone I could go to for guidance, but I knew, at that moment, what I heard was right. I knew I had to be around people that were willing to change and let their pasts go. My mother was not willing. Luke 9:59-62 describes Jesus' conversation with someone. **"He said to another man, "'Follow me.' But he replied, 'Lord, first let me go and bury my father.' Jesus said to him, 'Let the dead bury their own dead, but you go and proclaim the kingdom of God.' Still another said, 'I will follow you, Lord; but first let me go back and say goodbye to my family.' Jesus replied, 'No one who puts a hand to the plow and looks back is fit for service in the kingdom of God.'"** I know it is hard to believe that God would ever tell me to cut off my relationship with my mother, but the scriptures prove true. If I had not known the scripture well, what I heard Jesus' instruct me to do would have seemed crazy. God never asks us to do anything that does not line up with the truth of scripture. I felt comfortable that the instruction was from God and that it was the right approach to take.

In my life, God constantly looks for ways to turn this lion into a lamb. To hold a victim mentality for me is out of the question. Every one of my trials have been for a very good and caring reason – to remove a part of me to make more room for more of Him. Trials are not meant for punishment. They are not designed to bring on hopelessness or a sense of abuse. In fact, when God challenges us, we should rejoice. We are not victims but children of the most high God who is both loving and all knowing. We can feel privileged that He is taking the time to teach us His ways and to show us what works best for everyone involved.

The very most important quality of life is that we learn God's ways and are willing to obey and trust Him. I cannot stress this enough. Doing what He asks of us takes us from a mere earthly existence to living in heavenly realms. His ways are full of blessing and work so well. For example, if I had not received compassion for my sister and had continued to wave my sword, the end results would have been more devastating than if I had never shown up to help at all. Because I obeyed God's instruction, I was able to receive what I needed to give to my sister. Ultimately, all I wanted was to be able to help her. I had to realize that it was not going to be my way; it was going to be God's way. After all, it is God who truly knows what people need and God who knows how to best meet those needs.

Chapter 12
Be Faithful In The Little Things

Obviously, I believe that trials are our training ground purposed to produce healthy change. Sometimes they are there to teach us to trust God. Sometimes they are about obedience.

God gave me a clear vision to encourage my sister who became unemployed. I know my sister's heart and I am sure the vision the Lord gave me for her destiny was everything her heart desires. Many people want their heart's desires, but are not willing to do what God requires of them to achieve this end. Hopefully it is more about timing in her situation, and not because she is not willing to make the needed sacrifice God is requiring of her.

My heart's desire has been to be filled with compassion for all people regardless of their worthiness. In the case of my ailing sister, I had to put myself in a place where the Lord could use me as a vessel for that compassion. I had to live in North Carolina, hundreds of miles away from my husband and home for four long months. As hard as that was, I feel fortunate to have been able to be available for her. What good would I been to her even if filled with compassion if I was alone and happy in my own home? We need to ask ourselves if we are putting ourselves in a place where God can use what He has given us in order to help others in need. Are we just sitting at home praying for people? Do we ask God to use the abilities He has given us, but only respond if it is convenient?

Please understand. Prayer is by far the most powerful weapon we have. Faith without works, however, is dead. It would not have done my sister much good if all people said to her was, "We are praying for you." She needed someone to go to the grocery store for her. She was bedridden and was unable to leave her house for four months. She needed practical, hands-on help. If we ask God to use us, He will and then we have to be willing to go to where He needs us.

One of my friends was pregnant and her husband was sent away for six months of training with the FBI. During this time she began to have difficulties with the pregnancy and was experiencing premature labor. Her Doctors confined her to a hospital bed for the next month. What do you think I did? Did I say, "Oh, I am so sorry to hear about your situation. Just trust in God. He will take care of you. Cast your cares on Him. I will be praying for you." You know me by now. No! I took the keys to her car and told her not worry about anything. I promised to stay at her home and take care of her son for as long as I had to. We have to be faithful in the little things before God can trust us with the bigger things. Matthew 25:23 reads, **"His master replied, 'Well done, good and faithful servant! You have been faithful with a few things; I will put you in charge of many things. Come and share your master's happiness!'"** And Luke 16:10 reads, **"Whoever can be trusted with very little can also be trusted with much, and whoever is dishonest with very little will also**

be dishonest with much." Those of us who are waiting for God to send us to the proverbial African mission trip, need to ask ourselves, "Have I been faithful in the little things that God has asked of me? When a friend or neighbor needed help, was I there to help them?"

I am always amazed by my younger sister. She is such a great example of being ready and faithful to her calling. The Lord called her into the music industry. God has told her that she will be on the cover of many of CDs. She did not respond by looking for a record deal. God did tell her she was going to be famous, but she believes she must be faithful in the little things. Believe me, her initial shows were little. The first show she did was at a navy base fair. I was her backup dancer. We went out to perform and saw my husband, our sister, and two friends, along with three navy men. It was embarrassing. We were performing at ground level. Her song was called, "You Are Not Alone" and we could clearly hear the three guys saying, "We are alone." Ha! Humbling to say the least, however, my sister was grateful for the opportunity and did not let that show stop her from pursuing the vision that God had put on her heart.

Proverbs 29:18 says**, "Where there is no vision, the people perish, but he that keepeth the law, happy is he."** I have come to understand what that means. God gives us visions because He knows what we will have to endure in order to fulfill the vision. God does not want us to give up during the hard times so He gives us a clear picture at times of where He is leading us. A vision helps to keep us focused. God told my sister she was going to have success in the music industry, so that she would not give up in the hard times, and she has not. We have to prove ourselves faithful in the little things before He will trust us with more.

Chapter 13
God's Timing, Not Our's

God gives us visions so we will not quit running the race. A vision does not always immediately come to pass, if ever. Visions from God will not come to pass until God knows we are ready. Some visions take two years, as it did with my gym. Some visions can take up to twenty years or longer. Life, again, is a series of seasons and timing, which applies here as well.

As I mentioned in an earlier chapter, I would get a tremendous amount of pain in my knee. I do not remember when it first started. I just remember many years up until the age of eleven, my mother took me to every single healing church service there was in Florida to receive prayer for healing. Within the same timeframe of attending healing services, my mother would always ask me if I wanted to be baptized. In the sect I grew up in, babies were dedicated to God shortly after birth and baptized at a later age of accountability. My mother always gave us the freedom to be baptized when we were ready. One by one, my sisters and brothers were baptized. Every time one of them experienced baptism, I would have an excuse not to. I did not want to be baptized in the ocean. I did not want to be baptized in the church. I did not want to be baptized by that pastor. I did not want to be baptized in a pool. For whatever reason, I was never happy with the mode of baptism made available to me.

By the time I was eleven years old, I had been a Christian for almost as many years, but still was not baptized. My knee pain had not subsided despite many prayers for healing. It was at this time that my mother heard of a pastor named, Benny Hinn, from Orlando, Florida who had a significantly large healing ministry. Orlando was only a forty-five minute drive from our home. Once a month, Benny Hinn would hold a healing service; therefore, once a month for a couple of months, my mother and I made the trek.

At one such healing service, I remember it as if it were yesterday. I was wearing my favorite outfit - a white t-shirt that had two sheer layers of black and white polka dots on the bottom of it and a white skirt that had a sheer white layer over it. We sat in the very last row on the left hand side of the church. The church was filled to capacity, as usual. There was a man standing in front of me during the worship service wearing a grey pinstriped suit. He was maybe forty years old with blonde hair. I loved how he had his hands up in the air praising God. I said to myself, "I want to marry someone just like that one day."

When the worship portion of the service ended, Benny Hinn walked out onto the platform. I was ready to receive my healing. Benny Hinn said, "Today I am not going to be holding a healing service. Instead, I will be holding a baptismal service." With everything in me, my spirit almost jumped out of my body. I excitedly told my mother, "I want to get baptized! I want to get baptized by

Benny Hinn!" My mother informed me that we would have to sign up so I said, "Sign me up. What's the problem?"

"No", she said. "You have to sign up in advance. You don't have a change of clothes."

I did not care. I wanted to get baptized right then. Unfortunately, I did not. I went home sad and disappointed and that desire to be baptized by Benny Hinn never went away. It was planted deep within my spirit.

I am sure for years I would bother my mother about being baptized by Benny Hinn, but it never came to fruition. Every time there was a baptismal service at church, I would just say, "No, I am going to be baptized by Benny Hinn someday."

I was in my early twenties and I was still waiting to be baptized by Benny Hinn. Timing and obedience are everything in the spiritual realm. I was obviously too young at the time to understand what God was doing in my life. All I knew was that He put a desire in my heart to be baptized by Benny Hinn. So there I was, years later, still unbaptized, still experiencing knee pain.

One day while I was living in Connecticut at my sister's house, the pain in my knee was worse than it had ever been. I could not understand. I had been praying for healing for my knee for almost fifteen years. My sister told me about this man who was in town who had a healing ministry. Of course I went. Just like when I was eleven going to Benny Hinn's baptismal service, I remember this day as if it were yesterday. I was with my two sisters and our boyfriends. We are all now married to those boyfriends. We sat in the very last row of the seats to the far left. I was wearing a bright yellow turtle neck that said, "BEBE," in rhinestones and a pair of jeans.

The service started and right away people started experiencing healing. For the first time in almost fifteen years, I felt warmth in my knee and I heard the Holy Spirit say, "Your knee is healed." I was shocked! I could not believe it and was so happy to be done with this knee thing. Then the Holy Spirit said, "Go up and give your testimony."

I said, "No way. All I had was a little pain in my knee. People are going up there that were blind or deaf. I would look silly."

But the Holy Spirit said again, "Go up and give your testimony."

The only thing that kept coming to my mind was obedience. The prophet asked people to come up and give their testimonies. I slowly got up and walked down the long aisle making sure to go to the very far left of everyone lining up in the front. An usher came asked what I was healed of. I told him I had had pain in my knee for years and the Lord healed it tonight. Then the usher just kept right on walking and asked someone else what their testimony was.

I said, "See God, I told you it was not a big deal. I'm not going to get called up on the stage." Two or three people went up on the stage and gave their testimonies. Then, it was like everything started moving in slow motion.

I heard the prophet say, "You!" He pointed his finger right at me. "Bebe, come up here and give your testimony." I could not believe my ears. I looked up at God and smiled, while shaking my head. I could not believe I was on the spot like this. I walked up onto the platform and the prophet asked me what was healed.

I told him, "For many years I have had pain in my knee and tonight the Lord healed me."

Then, I cannot remember everything he said except for this: "You are going to be the next Kathryn Kuhlman and Benny Hinn." Never in the fifteen years of attending healing services did I fall down. That night, my knees weakened to the point that I could not stand up and I fell gently onto the floor in a state of shock.

To this day I wonder what might have transpired had I not gone up and shared what God had done for me, as the Holy Spirit had prompted me to do. The thought of missing the blessing of that night, or any blessing, because of my own disobedience really saddens me. I thank Jesus every day that the Holy Spirit nudged me several times to share my testimony. Later on that night, I spoke to God and expressed my total disbelief. I could not believe the words I had heard concerning my future. The Lord said to me, "That is why I put it in your heart to be baptized by Benny Hinn. I am going to baptize you with his same anointing."

I believe that any earlier in my life, I would not have been ready to receive the anointing of healing. I needed to learn how to be faithful in the little things, before I could be responsible for much. You would think that after that I would have hunted Benny Hinn down for him to baptize me. Unfortunately, that took another five years of trials before I would actually experience water baptism by Benny Hinn.

Chapter 14

Holding Tightly Onto God's Promises

It was August of 2009. I was sitting in bed reading the Bible when I came across the passages about Jesus being baptized by John the Baptist. I threw this out to Jesus, "I have waited twenty years to be baptized. I want to have my baptism like you in the Jordan River." At this time, Benny Hinn was a well-known name in Christian circles. He had a following of hundreds of thousands of people. Reading that scripture got my wheels turning and I wanted to figure out how I could possibly arrange to be baptized by Benny Hinn. I knew he conducted crusades all over the world so I decided to watch and see if he was going to Israel so I could sign up for one of his crusades. Once there, I would somehow make my way to him and tell him my story. Surely, he would hear from the Holy Spirit and want to baptize me. I can only imagine the conversation between God and Jesus. I can hear it now, "Bless her heart. She still really does not get it," they were saying as they shook their heads and smiled.

      One month later, I woke up to some exciting words. I heard the Lord say the words I had been waiting to hear for twenty years, "It is now time for you to be baptized." I was thrilled and immediately began trying to figure out how it was going to happen. I decided to research Benny Hinn's schedule online, but then I heard the Lord say, "Email the ministry." (Good to know God is technologically savvy). I thought, "Yes! I will send an email to the ministry and they will get back to me and it is going to work out that easily. Obediently, I emailed the Benny Hinn Ministry. My message said just this: "Hi my name is Cassia and I was wanting to know if Benny Hinn ever holds baptismal services. Thank you." The very next morning I got a response! It read, "Yes, Benny Hinn does do baptismal services. Once a year he takes a group of people to Israel and holds his service there. For more information call this number." I think I fell off my bed. I could not believe what I was reading. Not only does he hold a baptismal service, but it is in Israel. I called the number right away. The woman told me that the event began on November 1st. It was a ten day trip and included a baptismal service. I asked her if the baptism was in the Jordan River. When she confirmed that it was, I could not believe my ears. God is so amazing! I asked her if it was too late for me to book the trip and she confirmed that it was not too late. I ran downstairs to ask my husband if a trip to Israel in November was something we could afford. It came out more like this though, "Honey, I need three thousand dollars to go to Israel and get baptized. I will be leaving in one month for ten days." He said, "Put it on the credit card."

One month later I was on the plane to Israel. Can you believe that? When God puts something on our hearts, or when He asks us to do something, He will open the doors and make it happen. We just have to obey and wait. For me, it was a twenty-year wait, but it was well worth the wait and such an incredible lesson for me to learn. For the second time, other than the gym experience, I truly trusted God and saw His hand at work. I was learning how to cast the weight of the world I was carrying off of my shoulders and into God's hands.

When I think about my time in Israel, I am reminded of God's love for me. I cannot believe that God would put such a specific desire on the heart of a very young girl and then bring it to pass twenty years later. During those twenty years, many people acted so shocked when I would tell them that I had not been baptized yet. They would say I could not have been filled with the Holy Spirit unless I was water baptized. I got so tired of them casting their convictions upon me. I knew I was filled with the Holy Spirit, just look at all of the corrections the Holy Spirit had made on me within the last 31 years of my life, before I was water baptized. Only the Holy Spirit can correct us.

Does the Bible say to be baptized? Yes. Does it say to be baptized after you accept Jesus as your Savior and confess that He is Lord? Yes. However, God cares more about obedience than sacrifice. I truly believe that it was more important to Him that I stuck with my personal convictions about being baptized than it was to be baptized earlier in my life. I never said I was not going to be baptized. I never told anyone else around me not to be baptized. That is where being a lion helped. I never let other's opinions get me off track.

I knew that when I arrived in Israel; I of course would have only one thing on my mind - being baptized by Benny Hinn. However, as soon as I landed, I realized I did not want to limit God. I wanted Him to show me all that He had planned for me. God did not have me wait twenty years and have me fly half way across the world just to be baptized. I allowed my heart, mind, and spirit to be open.

I was so excited to land in Israel; however, we had to circle around the airport for about 45 minutes because of heavy rain. Once we landed, I boarded a charter bus with the others and we left for our hotel. On the bus, our tour guide told us that they had not had rain in the month of November in 50 years. They were having such a bad drought that all of Israel was under strict water laws. The guide said as soon as our plane came in it started raining so hard that they had flooding everywhere because the city could not handle so much rain and that locals considered this to be a huge blessing. The adventure began.

Upon arrival at our hotel, we were divided into groups. The groups were forty people to a bus. We were to stay on that same bus with the same group of people for the length of the trip. I liked that concept because it allowed us to get to know one another well. Right off the bat, I clicked with about six people. I did not comprehend the purpose of the immediate friendships, but as time went by, I did come to understand. God began showing me each person's strengths and gifts.

One of the first sights we went to was the Sea of Galilee. Looking back on it now, and recalling the vision I had at my sister's house of Jesus sleeping on the boat, I love to think how I was right there at the same Sea of Galilee where Jesus calmed the water for his disciples. The whole experience brought the vision and scriptures to life for me.

The next stop on the tour was to the Mount of Olives. Arriving at the Mount of Olives was another time the Lord brought scriptures to life. As soon as I stepped off the bus, merchants were trying to sell me things. Most of the people in our group started buying souvenirs. Immediately I started crying because I felt that we were grieving the Holy Spirit. I related the experience to scriptures when Jesus turned over the merchant tables in front of the temple. I really felt in that moment that I was living in biblical times. Obviously, this was thousands of years later, but I believe that scripture is applicable to our everyday circumstances and that we can ask God to give us the insight necessary to be able to apply them to everyday life.

Immediately I started to quietly pray in tongues asking God what He wanted me to do. He told me to just focus on Him this trip, to not be caught up in the tourism of it. As we continued taking in the sites, I noticed a crippled man, a native, walking. I stretched out my hand and started praying in the Spirit for him as I walked by him.

When we arrived at the Garden of Gethsemane, there was only one small entrance in and out of this very small garden. People were pushing each other in order to take their photographs. I was just overwhelmed with love. I could not believe I was standing where Jesus was betrayed. I could not believe I was standing where Jesus was so overwhelmed that he sweated drops of blood. I stood there and asked myself, "Would I have stayed awake and prayed with Jesus or would I have been like the disciples and fallen asleep?" I like to think I would have stayed awake and prayed for Jesus.

After I exited the garden and was standing beside the entrance waiting for our bus, something happened that gave me the sense that my whole life was changing. I had an experience that seemed to culminate and call upon the lessons learned in all thirty one years of trials. An older man with one blind eye was trying to sell me an olive branch. He kept saying he needed money to fix his eye. At first I said, "No, thank you," and kind of pushed him away. I was still annoyed by the commercial tourism. But he came back again. I said, "God can fix your eye for free."

He said again, "I need money to fix my eye." I said again, "God can fix your eye for free." He said it again. Then I said, "Money and gold I do not have, but God can heal your eye if you want Him to." I laid my hand on his shoulder and softly started praying in tongues. I was looking eye to eye with him and asked, "Do you want to be healed? He nodded his head yes and all of a sudden, almost without control, I grabbed his hand and started yelling at the top of my lungs in the Spirit. I was shaking uncontrollably. The man staggered back against the wall with a blank stare on his face. I felt like I was on fire. My entire body was hot. I prayed for about five minutes. Then I fell to my knees to the ground.

I could hear voices saying, "Be quiet."

This is where the lion kicked in. I said, "I will not be quiet." I continued yelling, "Jesus! Jesus! Jesus!"

The experience was so emotional and draining that I had to ask for help up from the ground and onto the bus. I was so out of it, I did not even know what happened to the man I prayed for. Later on I asked Jesus if his eye was healed. My right eye started watering profusely and He said, "It is." Remember, all of this happened before being baptized in water. I was definitely filled with the Holy Spirit.

Every time I think about this moment, I am reminded about the importance of obedience. I think about what might have happened if I had not waited to be baptized by Benny Hinn. What if I had been impatient and let someone else perform the baptism? If I had done that, would I have still wanted to go to Israel to be baptized by Benny Hinn? I believe I would have missed out on one of the most significant experiences of my life. I did not understand for those twenty years that God had more in store for me than just being baptized. Thankfully, I stayed the course and held to my convictions. It is so hard to stay the course when it goes against what seems to be the "law" in religious terms. It is even harder when what the Lord tells us will happen takes so long. That is where trust and faith are tested. Blessed are those who believe without seeing. If the Lord told me when I was eleven that it would not be until I was thirty one years old that I would be baptized by Benny Hinn, then why would I have the need to trust Him? Because I was only eleven, I know that I would not have understood what God was saying. God does not give us more than we can handle. Sometimes we think that we know what is best for us, but we don't. I am so glad that God doesn't listen to my plans.

We also are unaware of what trials will occur from the point in time that God gives us a vision until the vision actually happens. Thank God for that. I often think about Moses. God told him he was going to lead the Israelites out of Egypt. However, God did not tell him he would have to face Pharaoh and face several plagues or have Pharaoh's army chase and threaten the lives of his people as they tried to leave Egypt. When the chase led them all to a dead end, the Red Sea, what then? Moses had to believe that God would do the impossible. God told him to part the sea. The good news is that it worked.

Then Moses and his people had nothing to eat but manna for forty years while wandering through the wilderness. There was constant complaining and bickering, even murders and sickness. When those who survived all that arrived at the land God had promised to them, they discovered the land was inhabited by giants that would have to be conquered before they could inhabit the land. Here is the real kicker, Moses himself never even entered into the promised land. I wonder if Moses would have been willing to be the Israelite's leader had he known all that was to come. Perhaps that is why God reveals to us only small pieces of the whole puzzle.

So, when God placed the desire to be baptized by Benny Hinn as an eleven years old girl, He was smart to not let me know any more than that. Had I known that I would have to struggle through many more years of trials in preparation for the event, I may have conceded and been baptized elsewhere. Even the uplifting experience of hearing a well-known, reputable prophet tell me I would be the next Kathryn Kuhlman and Benny Hinn would still require five more years of trials. I may have given up if I had known what life would be like after my eleventh year.

It was during my trip to Israel that I realized God had more in store for me than just baptism. He had blessings and promises that I did not even know existed. Healing the one blind man was just the beginning of many of God's gifts to me during my trip to Israel.

Chapter 15
God's Promises Followed By Trials

God does give people visions. It happens. When it happens to me, my tendency is to assume that everything is all set. I always get plans in my head about how God is going to do things and that has been the cause of some of my biggest mistakes. I am naturally a planner and a leader and I like to be organized. For example, every summer growing up when we would travel to South Carolina as a family, I was always the one who would pack up the car and plan all the family outings. When I first acquired this role is unclear to me, but I have always been a strong leader who can easily design and execute a plan. This, in itself, is a good quality, especially for those God has called to be leaders.

For me, however, that quality has been a problem because I get impatient waiting for God's perfect timing and then I force events to happen according to my own timeline. I start trying to knock down doors that God has not even installed yet. It is almost impossible for me to wait once I have received a clear picture of what is to come through a prophesy or vision.

So, there I was in Israel and I believe God had allowed me to be His spokesman in order to bring healing to a blind man. Spiritual events were definitely happening around me yet it was not time for me to start walking in my destiny. I still had so many things I needed to learn. I am not saying that we have to be perfect in order to be used by God. I am saying that we need to be patient and that God will use us when He feels we have a foundation solid enough to do the job well. I misinterpreted the healing experience at the garden thinking at that moment, "Wow, this is it. Finally I am ready to be out of my cage and to see God's prophesy for a healing ministry come to pass."

I am so glad that God did not call me into a healing ministry just then because I would not have been ready. In fact, for three more years after Israel, I still had to go through significantly difficult trials in order to become ready. The issues with my older sister and her pastor and the experience with my sister and her kidney disease came after Israel. I thought I was ready; but, in retrospect, I clearly was not.

Think about Joseph in the Bible. He was just a child when the Lord gave him the dream that people would be bowing down to him. I am sure he thought, "This is great! I'm going to be a vessel for God." Again, like He did with Moses, God did not tell Joseph about all of the trails he would have to experience before God would allow him to lead a nation. His brothers wanted to murder him. Instead, they sold him into slavery. Joseph was then falsely accused and was imprisoned. I am sure he had his days when he thought, "What is happening to me and where is God in all of this? Did I just imagine that dream was from God? Is He really going to use me as a vessel and bring the things He promised to pass?"

A desire to be an ambassador for God is a good and noble thing. God has called us to be nobles, as kings and queens. God never, "Uses us," like a servant. I believe He walks beside us and with us. Thats not to say we should not have a servant heart. When we look back at the trials God has introduced into our lives, we can often see the purposes. He will begin a good work within us to refine us and to make us more like Himself. As Christians, we can know that difficult situations are not meant to knock us down. They are there to create a positive change in our understanding and attitude in order to make us more pliable in God's hands and to be more able to function according to His purposes.

One of the humorous things to me about the experience with the man with blindness in Israel is the fact that I yelled the name, Jesus, as loud as I could. For as far back in time as I can remember, everyone has told me I am too loud and that I need to be quieter. For example, one evening as a family, we were dining at our favorite BBQ place, "Fat Boys." I was a young child. A heavyset man walked in and I yelled and pointed with such excitement, "There's Fat Boy!" Innocently, I truly thought he was the owner and was excited to have spotted him. My family was humiliated.

There was another time again when I was a young child. My sister and I were riding in the front seat of a truck driven by my dad's best friend. He had a lazy eye. I leaned over to my sister and "whispered" to her asking why his eyes looked the way they did. I thought I was being quiet but then he leaned over and began to explain why. My sister was embarrassed.

My natural abilities do sometimes get in my way, but God made me this way. It is my job to keep myself in check. I hate when people say, "I can't help it. I was born this way. It's just how God made me." It is not right to use our tendencies as a justification for poor behavior. I think I have been quite forthcoming with proof that I naturally have many bold characteristics. That is how God made me; however, there is a place and a time for our natural abilities to be used. If we do not learn how to manage and refine them, it may be that God will never be able to use us as fully as He intended.

One of the reasons I felt compelled to write this book was to encourage readers to look at themselves honestly and to clarify their weaknesses and strengths. I wanted people to know that it is okay to make mistakes and to not be perfect. The point is that we need to look directly at our imperfections in order to define and refine them. Once defined, the weaknesses are easier to change, eliminate, or just learn how to live with them. Once we make the changes, we are more able to receive the blessings that God wants to give us.

Growing up, I was always a very happy and giving person. When I was ten years old, my family received a fifty-dollar, J C Penny gift certificate because we were considered a low-income family. While shopping, I noticed a young girl nearby whose family had also received a similar certificate. A photographer assigned to the event captured a scene of me helping another girl choose her clothes. The photograph that was later printed in a local publication clearly depicted my outlook. I remember not caring about purchasing clothes for myself at all. I only wanted to help her.

When a person is impoverished, there are a few different emotional reactions. That person can become bitter and angry or they can develop a desire to help others because they know what it feels like to be poor. I do not recall ever feeling angry about being poor. God always provided for us as a family. For example, I had an uncle that owned a very successful restaurant. Every summer for many years my family and I would travel to South Carolina, live at my uncle's house, and work at his restaurant. I started working there at a very young age rolling silverware and doing other small jobs. At thirteen, I started bussing tables. I enjoyed being able to work all summer and earn wages at such a young age. At sixteen, I was able to wait on tables and earn even higher wages. I worked all summer, every summer and always felt grateful for the opportunity. Working at my uncle's restaurant was how God supplied for my needs. I used the money I made during the summer to buy everything I needed for the following school year. Because my basic needs were met, I believe it helped me to never get angry about being poor. Living in poverty was not easy though. It was an ongoing challenge and trial in my life. I learned how to deal with it. I made a conscious decision to not blame God or my parents for an impoverished lifestyle, but to focus instead on the blessing of summer employment that God provided. Through my uncle's generosity, I always had a place to work and therefore never lacked the funds for the items I needed.

Because I starting working and seeing the benefits of hard work at such a young age, I developed a strong work ethic. God used the experience of poverty to teach me the importance of work. I could have complained about having to spend my summers working, but I chose not to complain. In fact, everyone in my family has excellent work ethics. It is one of the things I admire most about them. We are always the first people to show up to work and we are always the last people to leave.

Before marriage, I was in serious debt. My fiancé and I did not want to go into our marriage with excessive debt and we wanted to be able to pay up front for a nice wedding. My parents could not afford to help us with our wedding. Do you think I sat around praying, fasting, and reading the Bible? No. I prayed once and said, "Lord, I want to be debt free. Please give me the strength to work two jobs so I can get caught up."

At the time, I owned the personal training studio. I would work many hours a day. If someone wanted to work out at six in the morning, I would show up at six in the morning. If someone wanted to come in at eight o' clock at night, I would show up at eight o' clock at night. I would also personal train on Saturdays. However, that still was not enough to get ahead financially so I started waitressing on the weekends. I would have my last client at the studio at three o' clock on Friday then go directly to my waitressing job and work until eleven at night. Saturdays meant waking up at six o' clock in the morning to personal train two clients then arriving at the restaurant by eleven in the morning to work a double shift until eleven that night. On Sundays, I worked the same restaurant shift as the day before.

This routine went on for a full year without a single day off. The fact that I was able to do so showed me that God granted me the strength and answered my prayer. My husband also worked two full time jobs. After one year, we were completely out of debt and had saved enough to pay for our wedding. The strength that had kept me going for the year began to wear thin. The restaurant manager noticed and said he was no longer going to give me double shifts.

To everything, there is a season. That season was just for one year. Soon afterwards, I was financially able to leave the waitressing and singularly focus on the personal training.

I know so many people who complain about money and I always ask them what they are doing to change their circumstances. When they respond that they are trusting God to supply all their needs, I get a little impatient. It is true that God takes care of us, but sometimes it is through employment and the strength and ability to do the job.

I fully understand the difficulty of finding employment, doing the work, and staying employed. When we face financial hardship though, we should consider working. Ask God if He wants you to step out in faith and get a job. I know it can cause anxiety. Maybe you have never worked for anyone before and you do not believe you could do a good job or enjoy working. But that is the point. If you knew you could do it, then you would not need faith. You would not need God.

I understand now that God has used my most recent job to take away many of my natural abilities in order for me to need to trust Him. He knows that I am very independent. He knows that unless He strips things away from me, I would not feel the need to reach out to Him and ask Him to provide what I lack.

Sometimes the only time we reach out for God is when we are desperate so God allows us to reach that point in our lives to gain an opportunity to help us and to show us that He cares. I want to encourage you to stop worrying about having enough money. Take a step in faith and start looking for a job or two jobs. Just remember that everything is always just for a season.

Chapter 16
Facing Our Weaknesses

Despite my happy disposition, somewhere along the way, I started to have a problem with anger. The scary thing about my anger problem was that I was completely unaware of it. That is why it is important to keep ourselves in check and to continually ask God if there is anything in our lives that is not pleasing to Him. I was a teenager in high school when the Lord started dealing with me about my anger. Because I was stubborn, and too quick to justify my actions, I did not listen to God when He tried to show me that I was harboring a great deal of anger.

I previously mentioned the fight I was involved in during my freshman year of high school. I genuinely thought it was okay for me to hit someone in defense of someone else. Oh, God is so patient with us! He really does know our hearts. He knew that I loved Him more than anything in this world and that I loved others. All I have ever wanted to do was give to people and love them. That was very hard to do when everyone I met irritated and frustrated me. God knew my heart's desire and He was going to find a way to get through to me.

During my late teenage years, I experienced severe back pain. Visits to chiropractors did not help. As with the knee pain, I would attend every healing services in the area hoping to be healed of back pain. Similar to the experience with my knee, my back pain never went away. I could have complained to God saying, "Why is it that you will not heal my back? Why have you forsaken me?" We always have the choice of either feeling sorry for ourselves or submitting our situation to God and allowing Him to show us what we need to learn or to change.

So, one day I asked the Lord, "Why does my back pain never go away?" The Lord started to show me that the pain in my back was a manifestation of my anger. I never dealt with my anger. Instead, I just pushed it further down. I sensed that if I began to deal with the anger inside me, then the back pain would go away. Sure enough, as I started to deal with the anger, I noticed the pain in my back diminish and then finally go away. Because I was not aware of my anger problem, the Lord used the pain in my back to show me when I was angry and not dealing with the anger properly.

It may be difficult to understand why I did not know I was angry. I would get angry and then find an excuse to not have to deal with it. I would tell myself it was not my fault; that someone else was not listening well, or that the problem was because of someone else's behavior. I did not recognize myself as the one with the problem. I would say, "I cannot help being forward and direct. I was born a lion." We need to be careful with those excuses and to recognize that the very things we are using to justify our behavior could very well be the things God is trying so hard to change in our lives.

There was never a specific day when I realized that the back pain was gone. As I was careful to keep my anger in check, the pain in my back subsided. Ephesians 4:26 says, **"In your anger do not sin: Do not let the sun go down while you are still angry."** While it is normal to feel angry, it is vital to deal with that anger. If someone makes us angry, we need to either express our feelings to that person and work it out with them or we need to forgive them. The point is that anger is acceptable and expected, but unhealthy if it is allowed to fester.

Clearly, not all people with back pain have an anger issue. That was a personal conviction from the Lord, as many convictions are. The direction given to us personally is not necessarily meant for everyone. In other words, we should not try to force others to heed to our beliefs on certain issues.

I did not know at the time that God was going to use my back pain to teach me how to help other people be free from their pain. When I was in Israel, I was standing in line to check into our second hotel. As I was standing there, I felt this tremendous amount of pain in my back; so bad that I could not move. I said to the Lord, "Lord, do I have unresolved anger in me?"

He said, "No. The man standing behind you does." I turned around and there was a man standing there with his wife. She was bent over and obviously had something wrong with her. I asked the man, "Do you have any problems with anger? Do you have any unforgiveness in your life?" (Yes, I really did turn around and say that! This is where being aggressive and not caring what people think of me is beneficial. My experiences have given me the confidence to speak up).

Surprisingly, the man looked at me and very openly said, "Yes." He began to explain that he had a lot of anger towards his father and he had never been able to forgive him. His wife nodded her head in agreement with her husband.

I told the husband, "The Lord wants you to deal with that." He agreed and we both went on our way that was the end of our conversation for the time being.

In the meantime, after people saw how I prayed for the blind man, fellow travelers began asking me to pray for this same man's wife and to see if God would heal her crookedness. I asked God about praying for this woman's healing. Honestly, I had never prayed for anyone like I had prayed for the blind man and was somewhat confused about the experience. So while I hesitated to pray for her, whenever I walked by the crippled woman, I felt an anointing for her healing. When I walked past her husband, I felt extreme tension in my back again. I knew I needed to pray for them, but I was not sure what to pray for the husband. I knew that the pain in my back was caused by his anger and unforgiveness.

There was an incident as we were walking down a steep slope as a group and this particular couple happened to be walking beside me. I put my hand around the woman to help her. Her husband was holding her on the other side. As soon as I touched her, I felt an uncontrollable urgency to pray for her. She was very open to receiving all of what God had to give her. When I was done praying, I told her that I sensed God's anointing on both she and her husband, but told her that until her husband dealt with his past, she would not receive healing. It was so amazing to see God's hand at work.

At some point during our trip, the Lord asked me to go over to a particular woman and ask her if there was a scripture about unforgiveness and how it might prevent their loved one from being healed. Right away the woman started quoting several scriptures about how a person with unforgiveness could prevent his family from receiving God's blessing. I asked this same woman to share what she had read with the couple I had been praying for and we were all amazed that what I had felt I should speak to them about was also a concept that could be found in God's word.

    I do not know what has happened with this couple. I still pray for them occasionally. It is so important to be obedient to God. When He shows us something about ourselves that needs to be dealt with, then we need to deal with it; simple as that. Just do it! God has eternity to wait while we keep going around and around the same mountain or desert until we decide to face our faults. The good news is that God is showing us our faults in order for us to receive His blessings. We do not have to be perfect in order to be blessed; however, our obedience does reap some wonderful benefits.

Chapter 17
Finally Baptized

Returning back to my trip to Israel, we arrived at the Upper Room where Jesus had His final meal. My expectations of the Upper Room that I had conjured up in my mind for so many years were very different from the actual place. I thought that the presence of the Holy Spirit would be there strongly, but instead I felt a coldness in the room. I felt disappointed, confused, and sad. When I walked up the steps and into the room, I could not feel the presence of God at all.

I started asking silently, "Holy Spirit where are you?" My bewilderment prompted me to approach someone in the group who spoke Hebrew and ask her what she thought about the Upper Room. I told her I could not feel the Holy Spirit's presence. She read to me the words written in the stained glass windows. She told me they were Muslim inscriptions and confirmed that Muslims had taken over the rights to this tourist location.

Instantly, I fell to the ground and started wailing and praying aloud. I heard voices saying, "Be quiet," but refused and instead yelled, "Jesus! Jesus! Jesus!" Then I became quiet and heard someone on my tour bus start singing a praise and worship song. The entire bus joined in and the presence of the Holy Spirit filled the Upper Room with great strength. It was the most incredible experience ever.

When I think about that moment, I feel grateful that I did not let the opinion of other people prevent me from sprawling on the ground and praying loudly in the Spirit. There may have been as many as two hundred people in there, including many non-Christians. At times like these, being a lion is a good thing. Slowly but surely, the Lord is teaching me when to be a lion, and when to be a lamb. Surrendering my natural abilities and allowing God to develop them has enabled me to give Him all that I am and now He can work with me as He wishes. I allow Him to strip away more and more of my natural tendencies and as I do, I experience more and more of Him. God will continue to present challenges to motivate us to come to Him for the answers and changes necessary in our lives.

Afterwards, I was speaking with our tour guide who had led us to the Upper Room. He told me the experience was different than any other time he had taken a tour group there. He said that every other group had been very quite. He had been a tour guide for ten years, was born and raised in Israel, and was a devote Jew. I asked him why he thought this time was different. He said it was because of me. He saw me praying and then he heard the singing and praying of our two busloads of people. As he was speaking, God gave me the words to speak to him.

I said to him, "God said you are going to be a general in His army."

The tour guide looked shocked and said, "No. Other Christians have tried to convert me."

I said, "Yes, but have you ever seen God's power until now?"

God had so much anointing for him coming out of me. I was not even touching him, but I could tell he was feeling God's presence because I noticed him swaying back and forth. I think the experience frightened him because He quickly walked away from me.

We never know how our actions affect someone else. We can cause someone to slip up or we can help someone to grow in their faith. I have that tour guide's email. One day the Lord will put it on my heart to contact him and see what he is doing. It is so important that you do not worry about what others might think. You should care more about what the Lord thinks. Do you think He was concerned as He moved through His day preaching the gospel and healing the sick? Remember, He is always watching you. The more He trusts you, the more He can utilize you.

The next day of my Israel trip, Benny Hinn was preaching outside in front of the Wailing Wall. A girl from my group, my roommate, and I arrived early and we were dead center front row. Benny Hinn arrived and started preaching. It was such an amazing atmosphere. We were sitting under the stars on stone steps and I felt like I was back listening to when Jesus was preaching.

As the service came to a close, Mr. Hinn asked us to all go up to the wall and pray. I walked down to the very end and put my whole body up to the wall. I started praying. There came a time when everybody was done praying and loading up on the buses. I tried to push off the wall and I could not move. People were saying we have to go, but I literally could not remove myself from the wall. I had to ask two people to pull me off the wall. It was as if my spirit would not let me leave. I could feel the presence of the Holy Spirit so powerfully. To this day, I do not understand what that was all about.

Finally came the day of the Baptism. My emotions were high and the experience felt very surreal. For twenty years I had waited for this moment. I had no idea what to expect. I could not control any of my emotions. I was standing by myself crying before the baptism when a woman in my group came over and asked me to join her in line. She had no idea what was going on for me at that moment, but when she saw I was crying, she said I should be on the video because they are looking for people who have a special reason for being here.

A camera man came over and asked me what was going on. I shared with him that when I was eleven years old, God put it on my heart to be baptized by Benny Hinn. I told him that someone had prophesied that I was going to be the next Kathryn Kuhlman and Benny Hinn. I explained to the camera man that it had taken me 20 years to get to this place and how excited I was to be there. The camera man left and I went back in line.

As I was waiting, I told God I did not want to be baptized by Benny Hinn; I wanted Him to baptize me. As soon as I got about four people away, I started shaking uncontrollably and speaking in tongues. Before Benny Hinn even touched me, I started falling back in the water. I could not see anything because I could not lift my head up. I just remember going back in the water yelling in tongues, speaking in an unknown language, the whole time. Then I felt a whoosh and I felt Benny Hinn's hand on my forehead. As I came up out of the water, I was still speaking in tongues fully unaware of where I was and what I was doing.

A camera man approached and asked me to share my experience. My response was this: "Not only does God wash away our sins, He fills us with more of Himself." I felt that God had anointed me with a ministry of healing on that day. I returned to the bus to relish the experience and try to grasp its full meaning.

For twenty years, I thought about what the moment of baptism was going to be like. I kept thinking about how I was going to make it happen; I had all kinds of ideas and plans. I am so glad that God doesn't always do what we ask of Him and cannot imagine how many blessings I could have missed if God always did things my way.

We need to lay down our will and ask God for His will. I always think about Jesus in the Garden of Gethsemane. What if God had responded to Jesus' initial request? We would all be doomed. Jesus said, **"Father, if You are willing, remove this cup from Me;** Right there was Jesus's opportunity to walk away and not have to go through with the crucifixion. Fortunately for us, the rest of the scripture reads, **yet not My will, but [always] Yours be done."** (Luke 22:42). Hallelujah! Thank you Jesus for choosing God's will.

People experience a lot of confusion about knowing God's will. Certainly, God gives us freedom of choice. In the scripture I mentioned before, **"I give before you life and death; choose life"** (Deuteronomy 30:19) we see that God always gives us a choice. I told myself years ago that my choice was always going to be God's will. Jesus had a choice as well and could easily have chosen for angles to ascend from heaven, saving him from crucifixion on the cross. He was scared and faced a tough decision. Fortunately for us, He choose to do God's will and that has made all the difference.

God always has a will for us. He has a plan for each one of our lives. God cannot and will not force His will upon us though. It is up to us to say to God, "I want your will to be done and I give you permission to do what you want in my life." At that point, we must allow God to destroy our fleshly desires – those things in us that make us crave and drive us towards the things in our lives that do not correspond with the person God wants us to be. We cannot live to constantly satisfy ourselves and still be fulfilling God's will. It is either one or the other.

I knew for years that God wanted me to be baptized by Benny Hinn. I wanted it to be done God's way in His timing. I cannot say to God, "Let your will be done and this is how I want it done. No, it just does not work that way.

Once we proclaim to others that we have chosen to live by God's rules and standards, something else happens. We are now accountable for our actions. For better or for worse, we never know who is watching us. For this reason, it becomes important to demonstrate a lifestyle that does not lead others away from God's will or give them the impression that our actions do not matter to God.

When I was in high school I went on a date along with two other couples. After dinner the girls and I went to the restroom while the guys stayed back to pay the bill. The girls and I lingered in the restaurant lobby until we saw the guys coming. Then we all climbed onto our SUV and headed towards home. We were about thirty miles away from our home town when the guys started laughing. We asked what was so funny and they informed us that they left the restaurant without paying the bill. I was furious and could not believe they would do such a thing. They said they did not plan it; it just happened. That seemed unlikely, but, whatever the truth was, I still did not know what to do. I eventually told them to turn around so we could pay the bill, but they were to embarrassed to go back. Two days later, I get a phone call from the restaurant. The manager reported that someone in the restaurant had recognized me and given him my number. He asked that we come back and pay the bill and said he would not press charges if we complied.

You see, you never know who is watching you. If you call yourself a Christian, then you are going to be held at a higher standard of accountability. If you are called to be a leader, then you will be held at an even higher level of accountability. **"To whom much is given, much is required."** (Luke 12:48).

I was actually glad that the manager called me. I felt anxious about the situation. I called my date at the time and told him and the other two guys that they needed to go back and pay the bill. They paid the bill and that was the last time I ever went on a date with him. My choice.

Chapter 18
God's Unconditional Love

Most people think that they have to act like a "good Christian" in order for God to love them. The truth is that God loves us no matter what we do. He loves us unconditionally. When I talk about being obedient in order to receive blessings, I am not talking about being obedient in order to receive God's love. His love is always with us and it never fails. We can cloud our vision of that love by refusing to accept our situation, by refusing to admit that we have made mistakes, or by considering ourselves to be victims in life. Knowing God loves us can give us the ability to see our lives through His eyes helping us to avoid the pitfalls of clouded vision. Because God loves us, we can face life more directly, more honestly, and without feeling sorry for ourselves.

As children of God, there is a good purpose for everything we face. For example, I prayed for years that God would help me feel true compassion for others. Finally, during the time of my sister's kidney transplant, God used that trial to help me learn how to be a compassionate person. In order to learn how be compassionate, I had to be willing to put my sword down, stop fighting, and make an effort to see a situation from a different perspective.

God also used my father to teach me about compassion. In the beginning of this book, I mentioned that my father would act like a Christian outside of the home; but at home, he would be extremely unkind to his family. I remember feeling so frustrated by him. I could not understand how he could get on his soapbox proselytizing about Jesus, and then act so violently towards us behind closed doors. I clearly remember asking God to help me not become like him. That is what motivated me to pray continually for compassion. I assumed that as a compassionate person, I could not become a violent person.

There was a day when I was in my late twenties that my father was violently out of control. I could not tolerate his behavior any longer. I wanted to punch him. Instead, I prayed to God saying, "God, please help me to love him." I did not understand at the time how God was going to use my father, as He used my sister, to help me gain the compassion I was seeking. I very clearly heard the Lord say, "If you can love your father, you can love anyone." The words rang so true. In fact, beyond the surface meaning, was a deeper meaning to me: If I could learn to love and accept my own father, I could possibly learn to have compassion and love for others that struggled with the same violent tendencies. I began to understand that loving my father was a stepping stone to being able to love all people more fully. God used my difficult situations to teach me about His love.

One purpose of this book is to show that life is about the decisions that we make, our reactions to our situations, and our ability to admit our mistakes. It is about opening our eyes to see our trials in a new light. Granted, we all make mistakes. Hopefully, in writing this I will help others become more aware of the importance of acknowledging their mistakes and the importance of being accountable for their actions. God is able to forgive, to help us move forward, and to help us become better people.

The following story is a real life example of the process of making a mistake, recognizing it, and then making the necessary corrections. I was working in a restaurant and for the first time in my life, my confidence waned. Insecurity was so unfamiliar to me. I could not understand why I was experiencing these feelings. That is when I realized this position was going play a major role in teaching me how to totally let go of all of my natural abilities and to totally rely upon God. I knew for sure I was going to leave the lion behind and be called upon to become a lamb.

The first few months of this job entailed running food from the kitchen to the customer and were definitely the hardest times I had ever experienced. I felt so lost and after only a couple of months of working there, I had already had a confrontation with the general manager. He asked me to stop working to avoid paying me overtime wages, but that meant that I was going to be unable to assist my co-worker with all of the side work. The situation did not sit well with my morals and work ethics. When I confronted him, instead of being the ferocious lion I normally was, I started crying like a little kitten. I barely recognized myself. I even had several employees come up to me and say I needed to be more confident. I could not believe what I was hearing. Me, need to be more confident?

In reviewing my circumstance over and over again in my mind, I started realizing that God was truly taking away all my natural abilities. I would have to lean on Him for everything if I could no longer rely on myself. This was always my heart's desires anyway, but I never realized how hard it would be. I always wanted to lean on God, wanted to do His will; however, I would constantly start doing things my own way. I felt relieved in a way that now I had to do all things through Christ. I felt I had no choice.

The next few months continued to be difficult, but I trusted God to help me. It was clear to me that my mission was to stay focused on work and maintain my joy. Restaurant work presents a very real temptation to get caught up in gossip, slander, lying, manipulation, cheating, stealing, and anger. If we are going to be God's mouthpiece and His hands and feet, then it will be in order to bring Him glory, it is probably going to be in a place where He is not already present. That could very well mean that our ministry will not be at a church where everyone basically thinks alike. I realized that working at this restaurant was going to be a vital training ground; that God was going to use the experience to teach me how to fully trust Him so that I could have a solid foundation when used in a greater way my foundation would not be easily cracked. I fully believed this place was my ministry, but I also still needed to learn much more.

After working there about seven months, I was promoted to being a server. It was a great promotion; however, I was just finally getting comfortable with being a food runner. If we truly want to change and improve, then God will keep allowing circumstances to change in order to challenge us and help us change.

After being a server for a month, I realized that the hostess was not seating me equally; the table assignments were drastically uneven and not in my favor. The number of tables assigned had direct correlation to wages earned and so this was a real issue. To clarify, I did not want more tables than other servers, I just wanted equal opportunity for each employee.

Unjust behavior is hard for me to accept. I am not perfect by any means; however, I do try to live a just life. Repeatedly, I watched the hostess walk past my tables with a group of people and seat them in another section. One late evening, there were only two sections open in the restaurant, mine and one other. The hostess gave the other server seven tables to my two and I had to speak up.

I walked over to the hostess and said, "Have I done something to offend you? I don't understand why you are treating me so unfairly. Why did you just triple seat, then double seat that section when I have had two tables all night?"

She looked shocked by my questions and replied, "No, I don't have a problem with you."

I walked away, but I felt angry and was still obviously very upset. I approached another server who, when she saw how upset I was, suggested I speak with the manager. I went to the manager's office and knocked on the door. When he opened it, the hostess was in there already. I walked in and immediately said to her, "I don't understand why you aren't seating me."

She refuted, "That's not true. I seat everyone equally."

"You are lying. That's not the truth," I said.

She reneged saying, "The people didn't want to sit in your section because they didn't like the tables."

I knew she was not telling the truth because I had watched the whole event closely and had never seen any of the customers speak to her. The hostess had called me crazy a few times and when she said it again, I said, "If you call me crazy one more time, I'm going to punch you in the face!"

She looked at the manager and said, "Did you hear that? She just threatened me."

The manager handled the situation well telling the hostess to stop her insults and to seat the customers in one of the sections that is closed if they really were opposed to the seating arrangements in my section. I said that sounded fair and the hostess and I walked out.

I was still angry. I knew I had to go cool down so I went into the bathroom to be alone. I started praying and felt that what I had done was wrong. Threatening with words is not the right way to settle a problem. I realized that I needed to trust God in all situations and that the battle belongs to the Lord. I knew that I needed to apologize to the hostess. I was still in God's training camp learning how to always trust my Shepherd. I no longer wanted to be a lion, but a lamb.

I walked out of the restroom, walked up to the hostess, gave her a hug, and told her I was sorry for threatening her. I admitted that I had no right to do that. She accepted my apology and she apologized for her accusative words.

To me this was the greatest victory. The fact that after only thirty minutes I was able to apologize to someone was a new record. In the past, it would have taken me months. I would have justified my actions refusing to admit I was wrong or I would have cut that person out of my life.

Was the hostess at fault? Yes. However, was I wrong in how I handled it? Yes. I finally started to realize the reason why God needed me to become a lamb. It was so I would be able to wait on Him to show me how and when I was supposed to be bold. As a lion, I would strike without hesitation and that was often a self-directed, damaging response. As a lamb, I could stop, think about it, and more sensitively and properly react.

In order to truly receive all that God is trying to teach us during our trials, we have to be able to look at our mistakes. Most people would rather not deal with their mistakes. Most people believe that the only way God can use them or love them is if they are perfect. We will never be perfect in our own wisdom and strength. Facing our errors helps us become more aware of what we need to change, but our sense of perfection and acceptance can come only through God's forgiveness. Consider *2 Corinthians 5:21*, **"God made him who had no sin to be sin for us, so that in him we might become the righteousness of God."** When we truly grasp that we are righteous through what Jesus did and not from what we do, then we are able to move around in life with freedom, caring less about making a mistake and more about fixing one.

I want to go back to the concept of having a victim mentality. When we wallow in the victim self-pity, we are not be able to get through the trials that are set before us. I was totally being victimized as a restaurant waitress. For months, I would sit back and watch the hostess seat everyone else but me. Her choices were affecting my income. I had a choice before me: to be angry with her and God and act upon that anger inappropriately or to believe that all things work together for good and to handle the situation maturely by speaking up and prompting change. When we faithfully act the way God wants us to act, then this scripture applies: **"And will not [our just] God defend and protect and avenge His elect (His chosen ones), who cry to Him day and night? Will He defer them and delay help on their behalf? I tell you, He will defend and protect and avenge them speedily. However,**

when the Son of Man comes, will He find [persistence in] faith on the earth?" (Luke 18:7-8).

God introduces trials into our lives in order to remove parts of us that are not in line with His Word and not emulating who He is. He needs to constantly transform us to make us more like Himself in order to make us more fruitful. I know that I sound like a broken record, but the concept is vital to our lives as Christians. We have to remove our way of thinking in order to learn God's way of thinking. Peace will allude us during our trials if we do not obey God and if we fail to do what He asks of us during the process. It is important to remember that, again, obedience does not earn God's love, but obedience does enable God's blessings such as righteousness, peace, joy, patience, and other positive attributes to come into our lives.

Feeling like the victim in any situation is not helpful. The question we need to ask ourselves is this: "How long am I going to let this self-pity remain?" It is completely up to us. When we are going through a difficult period, we always have a choice as to how we will react. The right response will bring God's blessings into our lives as seen in this scripture: **"This day I call the heavens and the earth as witnesses against you that I have set before you life and death, blessings and curse. Now choose life, so that you and your children may live."** (Deuteronomy 30:19).

The word, "Life," here does not mean literally being alive. Life stands for all of the goodness that God wants to give us: peace, joy, faith, trust, hope, love, and so on. Death does not mean taking our last breath. It means all of the things that Satan tries to throw at us to steer us off the path: sickness, pain, fear, loneliness, poverty, jealousy, hatred and so on. God offers us the strength, determination, and discipline to choose correctly. We can choose to walk according to the situation as it appears to be on the surface or we can choose to believe that God supersedes situations and will intervene on our behalf. His word is very clear on what He can and will do for us when we live according to His best ways. God always has a promised land for us. Sometimes it takes a long walk through the wilderness to get there. We need to check our attitudes and our motives constantly to get them lined up with who God asks us to be. The process can be long, as we ever so slowly die to our natural tendency towards sin.

To return to the story in the restaurant, I apologized to the hostess as I felt the Lord had put on my heart to do. Shortly after that, I noticed that I started to be assigned large parties. I was being treated a little more fairly. On Thanksgiving all of my tables were tipping over twenty percent. I kept getting large parties that were tipping very well and I started to make more money than I had made before. There is no way I could have made most of that happen. I know that God can change our circumstances. Typically, He changes them once we obey Him and respond to our circumstances the way He wants us to.

I could have easily done nothing about my situation. I could have complained to God about not being treated fairly. I could have let myself believe I was a victim and harbored blame for the person who hurt me. If I had continued to do any of that though, I would have: (1) been fixated on that person (2) solved absolutely nothing (3) not given God a chance to do anything to help me. As our eyes remain on God and we continue to search our hearts, then we will be able to experience change. We cannot see our lives change if we are not willing to change them and the best way to do this is with God's guidance.

I had to realize that it was wrong for me to want to use violence to deal with my problem. I was experiencing anger and negative emotions. That response was everything I said I would never do. That is how my father would have responded. I would have looked like a hypocritical Christian just like him. I took the time to pray, and I knew immediately what I had to do to correct my situation. I went out on a limb asking the hostess for forgiveness, but I trusted that God's solution was the best solution and in the end, it was.

Sometimes our own actions or choices have caused our bad situations.

Other times, bad situations are not our fault at all. Consider circumstances such as rape, abuse, burglary, sickness, or an accident to name a few. In many cases, fault is irrelevant. My consideration has been directed towards those of us who had a choice presented to us and made an unwise choice. However, even if a situation is not our fault, we still have the option to decide to stop blaming the one who hurt us and ask God what our next step is for His divine guidance.

Chapter 19
Fear and Faith Contradict

One day as I was heading out the door for work, I receive a phone call from my sister with the replaced kidneys. She was speaking with complete terror in her voice and I thought I heard her say that her seven year old daughter had been in a fatal accident. I thought I was going to pass out. "What? She is dead?" I kept telling her to calm down and when nothing else worked, I knew I had to pray with her and ask God to help her calm down. I started praying for peace and telling her that God was in control. She calmed down enough to explain that my niece was alive, but in the Intensive Care Unit at the local hospital.

My niece lives in the mountains of North Carolina and the roads in their neighborhood are quite steep. She was out riding her bicycle with a friend and her parents when she started going down a steep incline. Her speed increased to the point where she lost control and the bicycle hit a curb. She was thrown head first over the handlebars and slammed face first into a fire hydrant breaking every bone in her face. She had broken her eye sockets, both cheek bones, her nose, and eight of her permanent upper and lower teeth were knocked out. Doctors had to sew her gums to the top of her mouth because she had demolished all of the jaw structure that held her gums and teeth in her mouth.

Throughout my shift at work, I was constantly texted my sister to see how she and my niece were. My niece's health was a great concern, but I was also very concerned about the effect this would have on my sister's health. I shared what had happened with my boss that night and asked for time off so I could be with them. He of course said yes.

That night when I got home, I booked a flight for the following weekend. When I arrived at the airport, my sister was there with my niece, who had just been released out of the hospital, to pick me up. Her face was still black and blue and swollen with her gums literally hanging by a thread. Even in her discomfort, when she saw me, her eyes lit up and she gave me a big smile. She had trouble speaking but still started to tell me a funny story. I remember thinking how amazing this little girl was. She was not going to let anything stop her from living her life.

My sister told me that while my niece was lying in the hospital bed, my sister kept trying to comfort her, but my niece who couldn't talk, kept trying to signal for my sister to not worry but try to get some sleep. I love that image. My niece cared more about her mom's well being than her own. She was only seven years old.

When we first got to her home she immediately clung to my side. I could clearly see the toll this had taken on my sister and knew I had to offer her, not my niece, strength and faith. My niece just needed love. I began to recognize the significance of the scriptures about being a part of the body of Christ. When one is down, the other is there to be an encouragement. We really need to keep ourselves open for the opportunity to use our own strength and faith for those without.

I was there for three days. Although my niece never left my side, I was so inspired by her faith. I thought I was there to help her, but in reality, she was there to show me what true faith is. Even though for four weeks, she was only allowed to consume liquids, she never felt like a victim. One night everyone was eating pizza in front of my niece and someone replied, "I won't eat pizza if you can't eat pizza." However, my niece responded, "I don't care if you eat pizza, my mom said whenever I am allowed to eat solid foods again, I can eat what ever I want."

I love that response she was not looking at her trial through the eyes of a victim, she was looking at it through the eyes of faith. She was trusting her mom. She knew that what ever her mom said, her mom would do. How much more will God's words come to pass if we trust Him?

I slept with her every night and I laid with her during the day while she slept. I knew that she needed the comfort and security that her parents could not provide. They felt overwhelmed and afraid. I could see the fear in their eyes. Having just been through the medical surgeries, having to face yet another tragic event in their lives was more than they felt they could bear. But I also knew that fear squelches faith. My sister needed someone who had the faith to tell her it was going to be okay.

What are we willing to do for God? Not everything He calls us to do is glamorous; not all of it is easy. I did not like the expense of the flight. I did like having to change my whole work schedule. I did not want to leave my husband. However, I did not want to leave my family to fend for themselves either. What is the point of belonging to a body of Christ if we are not there for each other when they have a need? Sacrifice comes with a price, but I believe the price is worthwhile. When others are going through hard times and may feel overwhelmed with emotions, we can stand in the gap for them and provide someone to lean on until they feel stronger. Just as Jesus stands in the Gap for us.

My niece's hardships will, unfortunately, continue until her facial structure is completely grown at about sixteen years of age. At that point, she will finally be able to have permanent teeth implants. Until then, she will have to be in and out of surgeries and forced to wear dentures. However, she is constantly telling jokes to anyone who will listen, sharing hilarious stories, riding her bike, playing outside with friends, and letting everyone know that when she grows up she is going to be the President of the United States.

Early one morning I was woken by the text, "Please pray right now that they are able to put a central line in my new born son. They are going to try to do it any minute. They tried last night and were unsuccessful. If they can't get it, they want to send him to Yale. We need a miracle!!!!"

I received this text message from my close friend who had delivered a baby six weeks early. The infant was unable to eat on his own. The insertion of a central line was necessary in order to supply his body with food. As with my niece's accident, the Lord used my friend's trial to teach me about the role of the church body.

In response to this panicked text, the first thing that came to my mind was the need to pray. As I was saying this to myself, I was hurrying around my bedroom trying to get dressed so I could meet my friend at the hospital. Even though I knew I needed to pray, I was experiencing too much anxiety to slow down enough to focus. You would have thought I would have learned from my niece's trial what I needed to do. However, the Lord is always still working on me. My mind and heart were racing.

I finally was ready to go. As I was driving, I heard the Lord say to me, "You can't have faith and fear." I thought, "Wow, that's absolutely true. I can not have both. If I do not have faith, then what is the point of praying?" I knew I had to get rid of my fear and anxiety in order to have a truly powerful prayer.

I asked the Lord, "How do I get rid of the fear?" He replied, "Whatever you focus on will become big in your sights. If you focus on the baby and his situation, then that will become big. If you focus on me, then I will become big." I registered the truth of those words and decided to turn on my praise and worship music in my car. Within minutes, I felt more focused on God. My fear and anxiety were gone and I felt completely at peace. Feeling peaceful enabled me to have the faith I needed to start praying for the baby.

As I continued to drive towards the hospital, the Lord showed me a vision of the disciples on the boat with Jesus during the storm. I felt the fear in the disciples and their doubt. Then I saw Jesus peacefully sleeping. The disciples woke him up saying, **"Teacher, don't you care if we drown? He got up, rebuked the wind and said to the waves, 'Quiet! Be still!' Then the wind died down and it was completely calm."** (Mark 4:38-39).

This scripture is a perfect example of how fearfulness can prevent us from praying powerfully. The disciples' fear prevented them from praying to calm the storm themselves. They mistook Jesus' peace for lack of caring. Jesus was not afraid. He was peaceful and had enough faith to calm the storm. I believe God gave me this vision as a confirmation of what He had told me earlier about fear and faith being in conflict. Seeing this vision encouraged my faith even more. Then I heard the Lord speak the words, "It is finished." Immediately, I knew that the Lord had heard my prayer and the baby was going to be fine.

I arrived at the hospital and met my friend and her husband in the parking lot. I shared with them my spiritual experience on the drive to the hospital. They were grateful for the encouraging words.

We went up the Neonatal Intensive Care Unit. The nurses asked us to wait in a waiting room while the doctors operated on the baby. After waiting thirty minutes, a nurse walked in and said, "The Doctors are finished. You can see your baby now." As soon as I heard the word, "finished," I knew that it was God confirming that He was in control.

However, next three weeks after that procedure deeply tested my faith. Although the baby's medical procedure was successful, each day following was a battle; the baby was experiencing one medical challenge after another. He was eventually transported to another hospital for more specialized care. The hospital was over an hour away from the baby's parents, increasing the difficulty of their situation. They were struggling as they watched their infant go through such agonizing procedures. It was hard for all of us to understand why God was allowing so many difficulties in the life of an innocent child.

I could not help challenging God asking, "You told me it was finished, Lord?" I speak up about how hardships have purpose, how you are in control, and how you use trials to help us grow. As I watch my closest friend go through this, Lord, how am I supposed to tell her that you are in control and that there is a purpose in all of this? This is her precious little baby, Lord. What am I supposed to say to her to encourage her?" I was frustrated.

The only words that kept going through my mind were, "It is finished." I called my friend often to remind her of these words and she would always respond, "Lord, you are in control." Together, we continued to say these positive words day after day.

One day while the baby was still in the hospital, the Lord reminded me of His words to His disciples before they got into a boat, **"Let us go over to the other side."** (Mark 4:36). Jesus told them what their outcome was going to be. He told them they would make it to the other side. Jesus knew there was going to be a storm. He knew that their faith was going to be tested. He wanted to give them something to hold onto in order to help them maintain their faith so He let them know the end result.

That was when the meaning of the story hit me. When the Lord told me it was finished, He was talking about the end result. He was not just talking about the first procedure. God knew there would be more battles to come. He gave me a message to share in order to help us keep our faith and to continue to trust Him.

Just before calling my friend to share everything the Lord had revealed to me, I started thinking about the importance of having others to encourage us during hardships. I began to realize that even the disciples who walked with Jesus every day lost their faith. How much easier is it then for us to lose our faith? They had each other for constant encouragement; how much more important is it for us to have other believers in our lives to encourage us? I realized that this is the role of the church body. It is to encourage, to pray, to remind, to be present, to seek God's truth for others, to interpret bible stories for others, to hear from God and share His words, to be an arm while another is a leg, and to be there for someone who is feeling weak to lean on for strength and vice versa when it is us who feels weak.

My thoughts continued to the scene where Jesus was sitting at the Garden of Gethsemane. Jesus knew exactly what was to come. He had to trust His father. He had to exercise His faith. Still, even He was suffering anguish. The Bible says, **"He prayed more earnestly, and his sweat was like drops of blood falling to the ground."** (Luke 22:44). Even Jesus himself asked His closest friends to pray for him. Imagine that. The saddest thing to me was that Jesus had to wake them up three times to ask them to keep praying for him.

In the surrounding verses, Jesus' words remind us why it is important to pray for each other. **"Get up and pray so that you will not fall into temptation."** (Luke 22:40, 46). The Lord used these scriptures to help me remain disciplined about praying for my friend and her family. Even though I knew the outcome would be positive, I did not want to see any of them fall into temptation or experience doubt about what God promised He would do for their child.

Fortunately, I have great news, the baby is at home, healthy and strong. Just as the Lord told us, everything is finished. The trial is over and my friend and her family passed the test with flying colors. They did not waver from the promises of God and now have a testimony to share with others that gives God all the glory.

Chapter 20
Victory in the Work Place

Many people focus on receiving blessings from God. God definitely wants to be generous towards us; however, God does require something of us in return. He requires us to at least try to listen to the things He asks us to do and to be. Obedience is essential in order to receive all the blessings God wants to give to us.

Remember what happened to me during my sister's kidney transplant trial? I had to give up my sword in order to receive compassion. God is a giving God. To give a real life example, a good parent whose child refuses to stop hitting his sister cannot reward that child with an ice cream cone. That is just the way it works. It does not mean a naughty child will not be fed and clothed and loved. I am greatly simplifying the concept here, but the concept remains still fairly simple. Parents who teach their childright from wrong are doing so primarily for the benefit of the child. Following rules increases one's ability to reap the benefits that come from living what might be termed, "a good life." The benefits include things like healthy relationships, safety, the absence of guilt and remorse, and perhaps a more positive outlook and more successful results, in general.

Taking it a step further, are we not God's children? Is He not our Father? **"Children, obey your parents because you belong to the Lord, for this is the right thing to do. Honor your father and mother. This is the first commandment with a promise: If you honor your father and mother, things will go well for you, and you will have a long life on the earth."** (Ephesians 6:1-3). This scripture then speaks to us even as adults. We should listen to our Father who is in heaven so we, as adults, can continue to live a long life on earth and be blessed.

Trials that we face are opportunities to trust and obey God. I have had many experiences that commanded I choose either to obey God or to do things my way. My obedience to God allowed me to be blessed and to bless others. I believe that the previous trials in my life and all that I have learned from those experiences are what make it possible to now be able to choose God's way. It does not matter any longer how difficult the situation is. I know through experience that I am capable of obeying God's Word.

Here is another story: It was soon after college while at my job God had put on my heart a certain female co-worker to help. I will give her the name, "Katie." One day a group of people we knew, including Katie, were planning a party at a local hotel and were booking hotel rooms to be able to stay all night. I was invited to join them and decided to stay overnight too. I do not drink or take drugs and never have. I knew what I was getting into and thought I should stay to "look after them." That was very normal for me, as I was always delegated as the "designated driver." It was a mixture of men and women. The night got off to a great start. People were drinking moderately and moving from room to room to mingle. As the night progressed, so did the alcohol consumption. People were starting to get a little loud alerting security who arrived at one of the rooms to tell us we had be quieter. One of the girls drank more than she could handle and got sick. I helped her until she finally fell asleep. I felt bad for her, but there was not much more I could do.

    By three in the morning, I was tired and ready for bed. People were still drinking, but I decided to leave and head to my room. When I got there, Katie, who I was sharing a room with, was already there. She and one of the men we knew were sitting on a bed talking. I went into the bathroom to wash my face and brush my teeth and hoped he would get the hint to leave the room so I could go to sleep. I got into my bed and they continued to talk. They obviously both had had plenty to drink. I did not want to be rude, so I laid in bed looking at them listening to their conversation. After about an hour, they both feel asleep. I was thinking, "This stinks. I don't want another man sleeping in a bed right next to me." That goes against my morals. I decided I would just lay there and leave as soon as the sun came up.

    At about 4:30 in the morning, the guy woke up and tried to awaken Katie. He was telling her he was going to leave. I was thrilled he was finally leaving. I had not fallen asleep. But when she did not wake up, he laid back down. Half an hour later, he tried to wake her up again. When she did not awaken, he started kissing her. You can guess what happened next and I layed there while my two roommates had sex. I was so uncomfortable and it made me so angry. You have to understand, I do not believe in sex before marriage and so this experience was extremely offensive to me.

I was thinking, "Screw these people. I'm out of here." I wanted to get up and leave; however, the new me, the one who has gone through trial after trial started thinking otherwise. I recalled the situations with my roommates in college and how God wanted me to continue to live with them so I could help them. Instead, I had moved out and never talked to either one again. I did not listen to God at all then and so He was unable to work with me in order to help them. I remembered that God told me he wanted to work with me in Katie's life to show her God's love for her. Therefore, I made the choice to stay. I wanted to do things God's way. I asked God, "What do you want me to do?" Then I heard Him say, "Don't say anything. Lie there quietly. Don't move." That is exactly what I did. Finally, the person left the room and went home. The Lord said, "Don't say anything to Katie. Go home when the sun comes up." So when the sun came up. I jumped out of bed with my clothes still on from the night before, packed my bag, and left a note for Katie to let her know I had gone home.

I was still so angry and disgusted by the experience, but I was pleased that I was able to stay calm and to follow God's instruction. Now I had to ask Him what I was supposed to do when I saw Katie again. Fortunately, a week went by until I saw her which had given me plenty of time to ask God for guidance. I felt strongly that I was not to bring it up unless she did. When I first saw her at work, she started telling me she had dealt with serious medical issues that past week. I was listening and felt concerned for her. I did not express the emotions I was having about the hotel room incident.

Later on that day at work, we started talking again and she asked if I was mad at her. That was when I knew I had to let her know how I was feeling. I told her I was not mad. I told her that I was disgusted about being in the room while she had sex. She was shocked and her complexion became very pale. I thought she might faint. She had absolutely no recollection of having sex that night with that person. She was genuinely horrified.

I was so glad that I did not start yelling at her or storm out the night it was happening. I could truly see sadness in her eyes. She did not need a lion; she needed a lamb. My past had been so instrumental in learning how to handle moments like these. Because I had allowed God to use trials to change my heart, I was able to become the person she needed at that time.

The next time I saw her at work she told me how she had realized that she obviously drank more than she should have, was unaware of what was happening, and had true remorse. She expressed her desire to change her lifestyle and no longer wanted to drink. She began to ask me about God, so I answered her questions.

While speaking to Katie about God, another co-worker was nearby and overheard our conversation. We were talking about God and about the possibility of attending church together. The other co-worker was someone who God also had put on my heart to share the gospel with. I will call her, "Julie." Months before all of this, I had overheard Julie telling people that she could not tolerate "born-again Christians." Right away, I knew that God was going to somehow use me to tell her about Jesus. When I noticed Julie standing there listening to us speaking about God, I knew the opportunity had arrived.

Julie said to Katie, "You don't want to go to one of those born again churches."

Instantly Katie said back to Julie, "Of course I do. Cassia is born again." Julie could not believe I was one of the type of people she professed to hate.

Katie spoke up again saying, "Cassia is different though."

All I could think about was that I was so glad I had not expressed my anger with Katie. Because I listened to God's instructions and confronted Katie lovingly, a door of communication and trust opened to allow for our conversation to happen.

I was unsure and a little concerned about how Julie was going act towards me now that she knew I was a born-again Christian. Within a week, both friends wanted to get together for lunch and spend more time with me. God was establishing a relationship with my co-workers in order for me to share the gospel. Julie was not turned off by my faith after all. I was so excited to see what God was going to do with these women. We went out to lunch and had a great time.

The following day at work, Katie said she wanted to go to church. God used this horrible situation for His glory. I asked God what He wanted me to do instead of doing what I wanted to do; I listened to Him. Katie's life will be different from now on. I am no longer in contact with Julie or Katie; however, I know a seed was planted in both.

When we ask God to work along side with us, He is apt to send us where there is a need. It is wonderful to volunteer to feed the poor, give clothes to the needy, and visit the elderly. There is nothing wrong with that and it is very important. For some reason, however, that is rarely where God sends us. We also tend to think of a ministry as working in a foreign, impoverished land or as becoming involved in a program through a church or a non-profit organization. That also is not always where our true ministry happens. The Lord told me my work place was going to be my ministry and He also told me the same before I opened my gym, God uses our work place as a place of ministry. God can and will work with us anywhere.

I have a friend who owns a clothing boutique. The Lord gave her the vision to open the boutique. He also showed her that it was going to be her ministry. One day I was visiting with this friend at her boutique when a woman walked in. My friend and I started talking with her and we realized she needed some prayer so we prayed for her and then invited her to church.

Some people find it hard to believe that God would and could use a business as a place for ministry. There are not enough positions in a church environment for every Christian to work. God can use any place His children are as a place of ministry. Why not take God into your workplace? We create the atmosphere wherever We are. If we are careful not to force our convictions upon other people and are willing to speak the truth in love, the results can be beneficial to everyone.

Our obedience is the key ingredient for God to be able to best work with us. If we truly want God's will, then we have to do things God's way. My hope is that in writing this book, I am enabling people to look at their trials through God's eyes. I sincerely want us all to be more aware of the fact that God wants to give us more of Himself. He wants to use our trials to transform us into the people we are not. For me, He took an uncontrollable lion and transformed me into a sweet, loving, compassionate lamb. Not only that, but God also taught me how and when to be the lion He created me to be. My journey is not over. I pray to God that He will forever change me and use me and lead me from glory to glory. My life is finally completely in His hands. Or so I thought.

Chapter 21
A Lesson in Humility

When I watch the news, a majority of the stories cover recent acts of violence. I find myself thinking, "Thank you Jesus that my life is not like that." When I go to work and hear stories from my co-workers about the previous night's party and their excessive drinking, I say to myself, "Thank you Jesus that my life does not include that." It has been easy for me to view myself as somehow more righteous than those around me. I never really thought of my comparisons as a bad thing until the Lord revealed the truth to me. I thought I had conquered the personal challenges at my place of employment. Little did I know, God was going to use my work place again, for an even greater victory.

For as long as I can remember, every time I read the story in the Bible about the Israelites and their blatant disregard for the way God had delivered them from slavery in Egypt, I would experience a sense of anger and frustration. I just could not fathom how they could murmur, complain and become so impatient with God after such a miraculous escape. How could they not believe He was in control and would take care of them after all of the miracles He had performed? Did they not remember walking on dry land through the parted Red Sea?"

One day my husband and I were reading the story of Moses and the Israelites and again I experienced all of these negative emotions. I said to him, "There is no way I would ever had complained if I were one of the Israelites who had seen God do all of those miracles. If I had been there and seen a tangible God traveling with me by a cloud during the day and a pillar of fire by night, I would never have doubted Him. My faith would have been unwavering." I placed myself upon a pedestal believing I was maintaining a higher standard of living than others. In comparison to them, I was the righteous one.

It is unbelievable to me how often I say one thing and act contrarily without even being aware of my inconsistency. I have always been proud of the fact that despite multiple challenges in my life, I have never viewed myself as a victim. In other words, I have made a conscious effort to think positively and to see my hardships as a blessing and an opportunity to become a stronger, deeper and more well-rounded person. Heck, this entire book is based on that philosophy. I truly was shocked when the Lord gave me a revelation one night.

As in every company, there is always a co-worker that gets special treatment. Without fail, someone who does not work as hard as others gets the promotion others deserve. As I stated previously my income as a waitress is based on how the hostess seats my section. Unfortunately, I am not one of the servers that got the special treatment from the hostess. As I stated in the previous chapter, I thought I had conquered the mistreatment of the hostesses at my place of employment. Little did I know, God was going to use my work place again, for an even greater victory.

There were times when God gave me favor and I had great customers sit in my sections. During those times, I believed God was my vindicator; that He was on my side. As I was about to find out, it is always easy to trust God when things were going my way. Just as the Israelites trusted God when He protected them during the plagues. It is when things go back to "normal" or when things go wrong that faith is truly tested. I guess this is what the scripture in Romans 12:2 means, **"Do not conform to the pattern of this world, but be transformed by the RENEWING of your mind. Then you will be able to test and approve what God's will is--his good, pleasing and perfect will."**

The key word in this scripture is "renewing." The word, "renewing" means "to take up again." I have never been an alcoholic; however, I could only imagine that a person who is a recovering alcoholic is probably very familiar with this word. I would think that even if they have not had a drink in years, they would still have to wake up every morning and renew their mind to think, "Today I will not consume alcohol." In this way, I need to constantly remind myself to control my attitude.

Here I was thinking that I had overcome and gained the victory over complaining about the hostess' seating choices, but I found myself slowly slipping back into old behaviors. As much as I try to take survey of my actions and to keep myself in line, in this case, I was completely unaware. In comparison to my co-workers, I thought I was doing really well and experiencing much more peace and joy than others were demonstrating. I truly thought all was well until one night when I could not sleep.

I was lying in bed, wide-eyed, knowing somehow that God was about to drop a bombshell on me. I had had one too many of these types of experiences to not recognize what was coming. I remember saying out loud, "What is it this time, God?" The first words out of His mouth were, "You know how much you hate how the Israelites murmured and complained and dismissed all of the miracles I performed? Well, you are doing the exact same thing."

I laid there quietly for a second to take in what God had said. I started thinking about my conversations with other servers at work and started to realize I had been complaining a lot. In my opinion, I was behaving righteously, but I found myself asking, "In comparison to whom?" If God was saying my attitude was similar to the Israelites', then I needed to examine that about myself and try to improve. But I still was not fully convinced that I was acting like my antagonists, the Israelites. Remember, I am the master justifier. My reply back to God was, "But God, you never performed miracles for me like you did for the Israelites. If you had parted the Red Sea for me, I would never have doubted your abilities and would not have the need to complain." I knew the scripture said in Hebrews 4:16, **"So let us come boldly to the throne of our gracious God;"** however, I doubt my approach was what that scripture meant. I should have known that God was not trying to trick me. He would never say something that was not true. I am not sure why I always feel the need to dispute Him. He continued to show me how I was acting like the Israelites, first by reminding me of all of the miracles He had performed for me and then by reminding me of all the complaining I had been doing.

Going back a few years, after I had sold my gym, took time off to help my sister with her singing career, and helped my other sister during her kidney ordeal, the Lord told me it was time to go back to work. I had no idea what to do for work. My husband suggested I apply for a receptionist position at a local spa. I applied and was hired, but told them I would think about it and let them know. As we continued to think of other places I could work, we came across a restaurant. I felt that God was telling me to apply there. I absolutely did not want to work in a restaurant. I had worked in the restaurant business since I was thirteen years old and after the last waitressing position, had decided I never wanted to work in a restaurant again.

However, I always try to do what God wants, not what I want. I walked into the restaurant and spoke to one of the managers and asked if they were hiring. He said that they were not at the time; however, I could fill out an application and they would call me if anything opened up. I completed the application. Two days later, the spa called to ask if I was interested in the position which I turned down. I knew that was not where God wanted me, although nothing had opened up at the restaurant.

A couple of weeks later the restaurant called and told me that they were totally reorganizing the structure of the restaurant and offered me the food runner position. A food runner is a lower position then a server. I just looked up at God and shook my head, then told them I would take the job. The fact that they totally restructured their system in order for me to have a job was miracle number one. This also goes back to the chapter on timing. God's timing could not have been better.

The Lord reminded me again of another miracle. Fast-forwarding some, there were food runners who had been working in this restaurant for five years before they were offered a server positions. I had only been a food runner for eight months before the general manager scheduled me to start training as a server. I really had no desire to be a server as I was completely happy being a

...ner, at that time. But the Lord just showed me back then that He had a plan and I wanted to be obedient.

One month before I started working at this restaurant, the Lord put it on my heart to write this book. After working at this restaurant for just over a year, the president and CEO of a huge corporation came for dinner at my restaurant and sat at my table. I served him to the best of my ability. He came by for dinner another night and again sat at my table. This happened a third time and the managers had noticed that he liked my service and automatically seated him in my section.

One day my general manager came up to me and told me that the president and CEO had written him an email stating that I had one of the best personalities he had ever met and was an amazing worker. Right away I knew that God had given me favor with this person. I did not know why at the time, but I knew God had a plan. This was just another miracle God brought to mind.

One day the CEO came to have lunch with his daughter. The restaurant was not busy, so I had more time to converse. As we spoke, I suddenly mentioned to them that I was writing a book. I do not know why I said it. I just did. They asked me what it was about and then the CEO said, "As soon as your book is published, I will hold a book signing for you." I was shocked. Here was someone who only knew a little about my book and he already believed it would be published and successful enough to have a book signing. If that was not God parting the Red Sea, I do not know what is.

Unfortunately, I had forgotten the magnitude of what God had done. I had become too focused on what harm the hostess had been doing and on the poor management instead of focusing on all God had already done for me. I had fallen into a victim mentality. I was too busy feeling sorry for myself, instead of being grateful. The Lord continued to remind me of the miracles He had done.

From that point on, every time I saw this person, whether he was sitting at one of my tables or not, he would tell everyone he was having lunch or dinner with, that I was writing a book. One evening he came for dinner and introduced me to the people he was having a meal with who were the producers of several popular musicals. He said to them, "This is Cassia. She is writing a book. Do you know of any publishers?" They said they did and gave me their business card asking me to email them when my book was finished. I could not believe what God was doing. It was amazing.

Another time when this person came to have dinner, he called me over to his table to introduce me to a Philadelphia Eagles pro football player. He said, "This is Cassia and she is writing a book. The football player asked me what it was about and I began to tell him. I shared with him my desire to be a motivational speaker as well as a writer. To my surprise, the football pro told me he does motivational speaking during the off-season. He asked me to send him the rough draft of my book and said he would love to help me out. I was thrilled. God had given me total favor and even though I am a huge Dallas Cowboys fan, I still considered this interaction to be another huge miracle.

While I was still laying there in bed with the Lord reminding me of all of these miracles, I began to see that I had indeed been acting exactly like the Israelites. In the process of recalling all of these positive events God had arranged within a very short timeframe, I realized they were highly significant. It is so important to remember what God has done for us. There could be nine amazing blessings from God, but we focus on the one bad thing that is in our way and tend to forget the other nine amazing events.

The next time I saw the CEO, I told him that my book was finished. He was very excited and asked me to email a copy to both he and the
pro football player. I felt honored that someone as powerful and successful as these two men would actually care to read a book written by me. The very next day, I emailed this book to both of them.

I know it seems so obvious now, reading about my miracles so nicely typed up; but it was after I had sent my book to them and was waiting for a response, that I totally lost sight of what God was doing. Between the day I shared my manuscript and this night when I lay convicted in my bed about my complaining, exactly forty days had passed. Forty days of complaining and forty days since either person had read it. I think it is funny that it was not until after those forty days, that the Lord revealed my state of affairs to me since that was exactly how many days it was supposed to take for the Israelites to travel through the wilderness to get to the promised land. Because the Israelites did not change their way of thinking, it took them forty years. I was so thankful that God had mercy on me and revealed my destructive way of thinking before I continued to "wander" for forty years. I did not want to continue to act like the Israelites and have to wait forty years to reach my promised land.

During those forty days, the Lord showed me how much I had been complaining. There was a new general manager that was hired
about a month prior to my book being finished. With new management, comes new problems and I would find myself complaining to the other servers about the way things were being run. Then I noticed that they would all chime in and

start to complain as well. When God showed me how I was influencing them in a wrong way, I was convicted. I knew that was not how God wanted me to use my influence. He holds those of us who claim to believe in Him to a higher standard.

    I decided from that day on, I would not complain. I made a commitment to stay focused on all of the miracles God had done. I was determined to remember that He was in control and He had a plan for my life. I went into work the next day and told one of the servers that I was not going to complain any more. I told her to hold me accountable and if I started to complain about anything for her to shake me. She agreed to try the same. Throughout that shift, when she started to complain, I would remind her of our pact. She would just smile and by the end of our shift she thanked me. She admitted that her shift was so much better because she had squelched her complaints. I was so pleased that one of God's truths had proved beneficial to a friend.

    The next day I told the same server again that we were going to try not to complain again.
She smiled and agreed. Just after saying that, her boyfriend came up to us telling us how the general manager just finished scolding him in front of other servers and managers. He was furious and embarrassed. I looked at him and said, "Don't let them steal your joy." He gave me the biggest smile and high five and said, "That's right, I'm going to keep my joy." Throughout the night, I saw him saying to himself and others, "I have my joy!" That is the type of influence I want to have on people.

    Even though I am not like the people I see on the news or at work, I had still been acting very much like the Israelites, complaining and forgetting about all of the miracles God had done in my life recently. I had forgotten about His promises to me and about my true purpose at work. In my human frailty, if I do not set my heart and mind on Godly standards, I quickly fall complacent. The Lord started putting on my heart the story of Joseph during this time of waiting and of feeling convicted about all the complaining I had been doing. Not once did Joseph complain about his situation. Not once did he lose sight of his purpose or his destiny.

    The next two chapters look at two of who I believe to be the most influential people in the Bible; Jesus, of course, but also Joseph. I want to put in writing the life of these two biblical heroes as a permanent reminder of what my measuring standards should be. I believe that God put it on my heart to write this book and that He promised to help me write it, which has now been accomplished. I need to trust and obey God, just as Joseph and Jesus did, believing that one day it will also be published. I believe it will come to pass and be a blessing to many, many others. It is requiring faith just as the initial steps of writing the book took. Life is all about faith as we watch God's plan unfold. I believe Jesus and Joseph exemplify this truth more than any other two biblical characters.

Chapter 22
Victim or Victor - A Real Life Bible Story

I grew up attending church services. Throughout my childhood, I was taught the stories in the Bible. I heard about David facing giant Goliath, Jonah in the belly of a whale, Noah building a huge ark, Daniel trapped in a Lion's den, and many other stories. Somehow, though, I had missed the point of the stories - missed their true meaning. It was not until I had a closer, personal relationship with God that I was able to see what God was trying to exemplify with each story.

As far as learning by experience goes, unfortunately, I have always had to learn by making mistakes. It always took a slap-on-the-face experience to wake me up and open my eyes to see what God was trying to do. This is not the way God intends to teach us. He gave us the Bible and stories of others' mistakes and triumphs for us to learn by. I guess I have come by my knowledge the hard way. I am finally at a point in my life where I do not want to continue learning only by my mistakes. I can read stories about the lives of the people in the Bible and learn from them. Of course, I will always make mistakes, but now I am more focused on learning from God's words and less from my own stubbornness and ignorance.

The story in the Bible of Joseph is one of the greatest teaching tools on how to get through an extremely difficult time. Unlike all of my personal life stories, Joseph is a perfect example of how to remain a victor and not fall prey to becoming a victim. He is a perfect example of how to trust God as our vindicator. The story exemplifies much of what I have been expressing in earlier chapters and so I think Joseph's life experience is worth reiterating.

Joseph was loved and favored by his father. Because of this favor, Joseph was hated by his brothers. They were jealous. Joseph never showed any animosity towards his brothers. I believe that because he chose to love his brothers unconditionally, God gave Joseph favor in life. God recognized Joseph's good heart and realized He could work through him to reach others.

Joseph began to receive dreams from God. In these dreams, Joseph saw others bowing down to him. The events, of course, made Joseph's brothers even more jealous of him.

Joseph reacted to the dreams correctly, refraining from pride and arrogance. He simply went about his daily duties. At his father's request, Joseph went out looking for his brothers. His brothers saw him coming and, in their jealousy, plotted to kill him. Fortunately, his brother, Reuben, convinced the others to throw him down into a dry well and leave him instead.

As the brothers sat eating lunch, a caravan of Ishmaelites coming from Gilead passed by. Joseph's brother, Judah, said to his brothers, "Let's sell him to the Ishmaelite's so his blood won't be on our hands and we can make some money." So they pulled him up out of the well, took off his garment that was made especially for him by his father, and sold him into slavery. After Joseph was gone, they took his garment and dipped it in goat's blood to make it appear to their father that he had been devoured by a wild animal.

So, I do not know about you; but if I were Joseph, I would have started punching, yelling, and cursing at my brothers. I would have said, "Who do you think you are? Don't you remember my dreams? You will be bowing down to me someday, you fools!" Instead, Joseph remained silent during all of this. He did yell for help when he was in the pit, but he never cursed his brothers or felt sorry for himself. What thoughts could have been going through his mind? He had experienced the ultimate betrayal and yet, remained so calm.

Many of us have experienced this type of betrayal. I want to encourage any of us to remain in right standing with God, as Joseph did. God will be faithful to bless us in the end. We are not alone. Joseph's bad situation gets worse. He was taken to Egypt; and enslaved by Potiphar, Captain and Chief Executioner of the Pharaoh's Royal Guard. Amazingly, Joseph continued to trust God and refused to see himself as a victim; both of which are vital keys to obtaining God's blessings.

The scriptures describe Joseph's situation saying, **"The Lord was with Joseph, he [though a slave] was a successful and prosperous man."** Do you think that if Joseph was constantly complaining about being falsely accused and reminding everyone that he was the son of Jacob, that he would have been able to be successful and prosperous? No. Joseph deeply trusted in God. He knew there was a purpose for what he was experiencing and that he was going to have the authority someday that would cause people to bow down to him. That belief kept him focused. As with Joseph, God can give us a vision of who we will become. It is up to us then to choose whether to continue to believe God or to believe and focus on our current circumstances.

Joseph continued to please Potiphar and found favor in his sight. Potiphar made him supervisor placing all his possessions in Joseph's charge. **"From the time that he made him supervisor in his house and over all that he had, the Lord blessed the Egyptian's house for Joseph's sake; and the Lord's blessing was on all that he had in the house and in the field." Genesis 39:5.** Notice that God blessed everyone for Joseph's sake.

Even though Joseph was wrongly treated by his brothers and faced the trial of a lifetime, God was still able to bless him through others. When we truly trust in God, the limit goes even beyond the sky. With God there are no limitations. The only requirement is that we do our part. The way Joseph pleased Potiphar was by doing his best possible work.

Are you doing your absolute best effort in your work situation or in any situation you find yourself in? For me, it is a daily challenge to show up at work and not complain. It is a daily challenge to trust God to carry me through to a victorious place. Daily, I must choose to perform to the best of my ability, regardless of the challenging personalities surrounding me. Studying people's lives, like Joseph's, helps me make the right choices as an employee and otherwise. Joseph did not even have the help of the Holy Spirit like we do now. So, if he can do it, we can do it.

The next part of Joseph's life is even more frustrating to me than the first part. Injustice absolutely infuriates me. I do realize that the anger I feel, particularly when injustice affects me directly, is a lack of trusting God as my vindicator. If I truly trusted He were in control, then

I would not get so frustrated. That is where Joseph and I differ. Listen to what happened to Joseph next.

Potiphar's wife approached Joseph requesting he be intimate with her. As always, Joseph chose correctly by denying her request, keeping himself in right standing before his authority and God. Joseph continued to say no despite Potiphar's wife's relentless pleas. One day while they were alone, she grabbed him by his garment demanding a final time that Joseph commit adultery with her. Joseph ran out of the room leaving his garment behind.

Instead of God providing a way out for Joseph for having responded obediently and remaining in right standing before his authorities, the exact opposite happened. Potipher's wife was furious and insulted. She called to the men of her house and accused Joseph of trying to seduce her. When Potiphar heard this lie, he sent Joseph to prison. Still, Joseph believed that God was his vindicator. His behavior remained stellar in the face of blatant injustice and he refused to view himself as a victim in life.

When things like this happen to us, we have to hold on tightly to God's promises and trust that He is in control. If we do not, then we will become victims instead of victors. I am always so amazed at how Joseph never once viewed himself as a victim. That is why I love to read and think about the people in the Bible. Of course, Jesus is the ultimate example of who we should be, but He never sinned. Even though He faced temptations as we do, He never messed up. I rather enjoy reading about people with dilemmas who did mess up and had to learn from their mistakes like the rest of us. Joseph's brothers were full of the types of evils we see in our world every day. This is an old, old story that is as relevant today as it was thousands of years ago.

Joseph remained blameless in the sight of God. As a result, Genesis 29:21 states, **"But the Lord was with Joseph, and showed him mercy and loving-kindness and gave him favor in the sight of the warden of the prison."** Amazing, is it not? Even though Joseph is in the worst place known to humankind, God is still able to bless him and love him. The warden of the prison gave Joseph authority to take care of all of the prisoners. In fact, the Lord caused ALL that Joseph did to prosper.

God can do this for us even now. Despite the trials we are facing momentarily, we can still be blessed and bless those around us. What a remarkable concept! This is the definition of true love. We adhere to the right choices and those around us even get to reap the benefits. Honestly, I could not care less if my boss received any sort of blessing; however, I know that is not how God works. God has dealt strongly with me in the past about how by practicing the expression of love for my father would enable me to love others as well. I know that it is possible for Joseph to truly love the unlovable because the same thing happened in my life. That is God's type of love. God loves us all, right where we are, exactly as we are right now - no holds barred.

The next part of Joseph's life is always an eye-opener for me. As I mentioned before, I like to plan and figure things out. If things are not happening quickly enough, I get right in there and move the process along. What I love about Joseph is that his whole trial lasted about twenty years. I know that I would have become extremely impatient with God and perhaps would have lost faith believing that God had forgotten about me. Joseph continued to trust God and as a result, God was able to line everything up in order from Joseph to save a nation.

Most of the time, we are unaware of exactly what God is doing. We do not know how or when He is going to do something, even if He has promised to do it for us. But we have to trust regardless of how things look that He is in complete control.

At this time, Pharaoh was angry with his chief butler and the chief baker and sent them to prison, the same one imprisoning Joseph. That night as the chiefs slept, they each had a dream. When Joseph saw them the next morning, they both looked sad. I love this. Why would any one prisoner care if two other prisoners looked sad? Of course, they were sad; they were in prison. However, Joseph knew that there was something more happening and his love for others led him to reach out to the chiefs.

The chief butler and chief baker told him that they each had a dream but noted that there was no person present to interpret the dreams. Joseph responded by saying, **"Do not interpretations belong to God?"** (Genesis 40:8). They proceeded to tell Joseph their dreams. Immediately, God gave Joseph the interpretations of the dreams: The butler would be released from prison and allowed to return to his butlership. The baker, however, would be hanged. Joseph then asked the butler to remember him and to tell Pharaoh about the interpretation of the dreams.

God is lining everything up for Joseph. Keep in mind that Joseph never complained. He never lost sight of God in all of his difficult circumstances. He always trusted God and that trust gave him the strength and insight he needed in order to push through to the other side. When we truly trust God, we can have peace. When we have peace, then we will have patience. When we have patience, then God can work along with us for His glory.

The time came when the butler was released from prison and returned to his butlership while the baker was hanged. During this time, Pharaoh received a dream and was unable to interpret his dream. He sent out a notice to his people requesting the interpretation. No one in the kingdom was able to do so. At that point, the butler remembered how Joseph had accurately interpreted the dreams and told Pharaoh about Joseph's ability. Pharaoh sent for Joseph and like the time before, Joseph gave the glory to God and stating, **"It is not in me; God [not I] will give Pharaoh a [favorable] answer and peace."** (Genesis 41:16). Joseph interpreted Pharaoh's dream. Then Pharaoh said, **"And Pharaoh said to Joseph, 'Forasmuch as [your] God has shown you all this, there is nobody as intelligent and discreet and understanding and wise as you are. You shall have charge over my house, and all my people shall be governed according to your word [with reverence, submission, and obedience]. Only in matters of the throne will I be greater than you are.' Then Pharaoh said to Joseph, 'See, I have set you over all of Egypt.' Pharaoh took off his [signet] ring from his hand and put it on Joseph's hand, and arrayed him in [official] vestments of fine linen and put a gold chain about his neck."** (Genesis 41:39-42).

Joseph, in a single day, rose from being a prisoner to being a governor. Could this have happened if Joseph had decided to whimper and feel sorry for himself in each circumstance he found himself? I think not. I believe that various people over the years recognized something very different about Joseph. He had what it took to rule. God knew that one day he would rule over Egypt and each experience, though dreadful at the time, actually had a purpose. It was God's way of creating the perfect resume for the job Joseph would one day hold, Ruler of Egypt.

Look at it: Executive Director for Captain of Egyptian Royal Guard; Executive Director for Department of Egyptian Incarceration System; Special interests: Dream interpretation, 25+ years of experience with 100% accuracy rate. God was using Joseph's trials to teach him and prepare him to be a ruler over a nation. Because Joseph allowed God to guide him without complaining or feeling victimized, Joseph won the high position of ruler of Egypt. With wisdom, humility, and kindness, he led and saved a nation through its darkest years of drought and famine and was even willing and able to save his entire family (including the brothers who had previously wanted to kill him) from inevitable death.

Joseph's story is a great example of how keeping a victorious mentality during a hardship can allow us to receive God's blessings. It is always important to read about the people in the Bible to see all of their defeats and triumphs. Ask God to make them real to you. Ask Him to show you how you are similar to these characters. We are always going to have trials; however, we can always find someone in the Bible who has faced a similar trail. Look and see how God helped them. Look to see how God changed them and made them stronger individuals as a result of their trials. That is what I value most about the words of the Bible.

There is also the story in the Bible of David who lost his son. Like Joseph, David had to face many challenges in order to walk in his calling from God. Granted, I have never had to experience a death in the family or physical or sexual abuse and as far as I know, neither has anyone else in my family. But many have. If you have faced the severity of the above-mentioned events, I want to encourage you to find and read about the person in the Bible who shares your experience. I guarantee, it is in there.

To set the stage, David's baby was ill. **"David prayed to God for the baby. David fasted and went into his house and stayed there, lying on the ground all night. The elders of David's family came to him and tried to pull him up from the ground, but he refused to get up or to eat food with them. On the seventh day the baby died. David's servants were afraid to tell him that the baby was dead. They said, 'Look, we tried to talk to David while the baby was alive, but he refused to listen to us. If we tell him the baby is dead, he may do something awful.' When David saw his servants whispering, he knew that the baby was dead. So he asked them, 'Is the baby dead?' They answered, 'Yes, he is dead.' Then David got up from the floor, washed himself, put lotions on, and changed his clothes. Then he went into the Lord's house to worship. After that, he went home and asked for something to eat. His servants gave him some food, and he ate. David's servants said to him, 'Why are you doing this? When the baby was still alive, you fasted and you cried. Now that the baby is dead, you get up and eat food.' David said, 'While the baby was still alive, I fasted, and I cried.' I thought, 'Who knows? Maybe the Lord will feel sorry for me and let the baby live. But now that the baby is dead, why should I fast? I can't bring him back to life. Someday I will go to him, but he cannot come back to me.'"**

David's response may seem a bit insensitive, but he really did have a valid point. I cannot imagine the pain, guilt, anger, and every other emotion that might take place in this type of horrific tragedy. While our emotions are God-given and have a purpose, we can still learn something important from David's response. That is, there is always a time for mourning, and then there is a time for moving forward. There is a time for anger, and then a time for healing.

In verse 22, David had a victim mentality. He said, **"Maybe the Lord will feel sorry for me."** It is human to feel sad and hopeless and more than acceptable. However, once David realized that there was nothing left for him to do, he changed his way of thinking and began to have faith and hope. Reading more into the story, we discover that God was then able to give David a new son named Solomon who went down in history as one of the wisest men who ever lived. The question we need to ask ourselves then is how long we are going to mourn?

Suffering hurt or sadness is a part of life. I will never be thrilled about that, but there is no way to change that reality. The only thing we truly have control over is how we chose to react. Somehow, we must find the strength to believe God is going to use this for His glory and purpose. He is going to use this pain to change us and to somehow bless our lives. It takes a great amount of strength, sometimes aided by the help of others, to take our eyes off our pain and hurt. After our period of mourning is over, we need to focus on the One who loves us and allow that to help us get through to the other side, to a brighter place. We are never alone in our struggles even when it feels as such.

Chapter 23
The Hardest Trial of All

I have been very forthcoming with all of the mistakes, frustrations, ups and downs, challenges, and changes that have consumed the majority of my life. My reveal has a purpose which is to, hopefully, demonstrate how to overcome a victim mentality and how to see personal trials through God's eyes.

Throughout the previous chapters, I discussed techniques on how to let go of wrong ways of thinking; that is, wrong templates created by our natural characteristics and our environments. In other chapters, I pointed out the importance, not of being perfect, but of accepting mistakes as part of life and being willing to let God correct us. It becomes much more important to obey and seek righteousness than to ever be perfect. In still other chapters, I explained how I was able to let go of my natural lion-like aggression in order to allow God to develop other gifts. As I let go of some of the ways that hindered God from being able to use me, I made room for Him to reflect who He is in me. God was able to transform me from a rather ferocious lion into a sensitive, loving lamb.

In this final chapter, I turn the attention away from my own life-long trials toward the ultimate trial - a trial so fierce, so agonizing, so brutal, that it caused this person to sweat blood. He was betrayed by someone he loved and shared time with. He was wrongly accused and charged with crimes He never committed. He was falsely convicted and finally put to death. This man was Jesus. He hung on a cross for no real reason at all. And yet, he died for the greatest purpose of all. Jesus' death provided eternal life for every single man, woman, and child born from that day forward.

Here is the story of Jesus' final hours and His ultimate trial: Jesus was in the Garden of Gethsemane praying that perhaps God, His father could spare Him from what was about to happen. He had asked His disciples to stay awake and pray for Him; He asked for their spiritual and emotional support just as we would do in a similar situation. As He was praying in anguish, every one of His disciples fell asleep. His dearest friends let Him down in His greatest time of need. Sound familiar? This has happened to us all at times. The remarkable thing is that despite His deep disappointment in their apparent lack of concern, Jesus still expressed His unconditional love for them. His exact words were, **"Forgive them, Father, for they know not what they do."** (Luke 23:34).

As He was praying fervently, guards showed up in the Garden to arrest Him. One of His own beloved disciples had led His captors directly to Him. Jesus had been betrayed. Imagine what that might feel like to have our best friend turn his back, causing our death in return for just a small amount of money.

Jesus then had to go on trial for crimes He never committed. He had to stand alone in front of a mob of angry, unjust people to learn of His fate. Jesus already knew what the outcome would be. Pilate, who was the deciding authority, said to the mob, **"'Whom do you want me to set free for you, Barabbas, or Jesus Who is called Christ?' But the chief priests and the elders prevailed on the people to ask for Barabbas, and put Jesus to death. Again the governor said to them, 'Which of the two do you wish me to release for you?' And they said, 'Barabbas!' Pilate said to them, 'Then what shall I do with Jesus who is called Christ?' They all replied, 'Let Him be crucified!' And he said, 'Why? What has He done that is evil?' But they shouted all the louder, 'Let Him be crucified!'"** (Matthew 27:17, 20-23). Pilate did as the mob demanded. Just as Joseph was wrongly accused, Jesus was wrongly accused. However, Jesus knew that His father was in control. Jesus knew that this was the entire purpose for coming to earth.

If anyone had the right to have a victim mentality, it was Jesus. Every one of us, including Jesus has a choice on how they are going to respond to their trials. We can choose to see our situation as a stepping stone to something greater or as a pitfall. As a warning, oftentimes our attitude creates the outcome, however; Jesus chose to believe that His outcome would be to enter into the fullness of God and all of His blessings.

Although God was fully in control of Jesus' circumstance and Jesus made the correct choice to obey, the trial was still not over for Jesus. He proceeded to be whipped and stripped of His clothing. To mock His proclamation that He was the Messiah sent by God, the governor's soldiers dressed Jesus in a royal, scarlet robe and placed a crown of thorns on His head. Placing a reed in His right hand, the soldiers knelt before Him and said sarcastically, **"Hail, King of the Jews!"** (Matthew 27:29).

The humiliation continued as the soldiers spit on Him and struck His head with their staffs. When they were finished, they stripped Him of His robe, put Him back in His own garments and lead Him away to be crucified.

My stomach turns every time I think about what was done to Him. I understand that Jesus had to die on the cross in order to take away our sins so that we could be redeemed; however, I do not understand why it had to be so torturous. It was hard enough to have to be hung on a cross. The way He died and the noble way He acted throughout the experience causes me to love Jesus more and more each time I think about His ordeal.

One would think that Jesus' trial was over; it was not. The mocking continued while He hung on the cross dying. While Jesus was hanging on the cross, He had to face the deepest feeling of abandonment. His own father, God, who sent Him down to earth to die for mankind, became silent. **"And about the ninth hour Jesus cried with a loud voice, 'Eli, Eli, Iama sabachthani? - that is, My God, My God, why have you abandoned me?'"** (Matthew 27:46). Jesus felt abandoned by even His own Father.

Jesus had to face so many hardships during His time on earth. Who are we to think that we should not have any hardships? The question should never be, "Why, God, why me?" It should be instead, "What? What are you trying to teach me? What are you trying to be for me at this moment?"

We will all have trials throughout our lives. It is a given. Our purpose and goal should be, not to avoid or become victim to our difficulties, but to learn how to respond correctly to the challenges we face. We should respond in a way that allows us to get rid of our selfish nature and to receive more of God's nature. In the long run,

God is working with us for our benefit, not His. This takes some huge level of trust at times though to believe. God understands that.

Like Joseph, Jesus responded according to the will of God. My favorite passages in the entire Bible are found just before the crucifixion. It happened when Jesus had a choice of whether or not to go through this turmoil. **"And going a little farther, He threw Himself upon the ground on His face and prayed saying, 'My Father, if it is possible, let this cup pass away from Me; Nevertheless, not what I will, but as You will and desire.'" And He came to the disciples and found them sleeping, and He said to Peter, 'What! Are you so utterly unable to stay awake and keep watch with Me for one hour? All of you must keep awake and watch and pray, that you may not come into temptation. The spirit indeed is willing, but the flesh is weak.' Again a second time He went away and prayed, 'My Father, if this cannot pass by unless I drink it, Your will be done.' And again He came and found them sleeping, for their eyes were weighed down with sleep. So, leaving them again, He went away and prayed for the third time, using the same words." (Matthew 26:39-44)**

How remarkable is Jesus? Three times He asked God if it was possible to take his trial away from Him. Three times! Each time, Jesus ended His prayer by saying, "Not my will Father, but Yours." Oh, that we could have that much faith and trust in God enough to proclaim in the midst of our trials, "Not my will, but Yours."

Reading the Bible and asking the Holy Spirit for the revelation of the words is key to having victory in our lives. It is through reading these stories that our faith is strengthened. **"So then faith comes by hearing, and hearing by the word of God."** (Romans 10:17)

I want to finish with one last thought: Faith, hope, and love are the three qualities that will help us to get through our trials. These are the fruits of a righteous walk. A righteous walk is obtained by knowing we are righteous not by our works, but by the blood that was shed by Jesus. He was the ultimate sacrifice accepted by God as the full forgiveness for all of our sins. **2 Corinthians 5:21 says, "For he has made him [to be] sin for us, who knew no sin; that we might be made the righteousness of God in him."**

How do we receive faith, hope, and love? It is by knowing who Jesus is. It is by knowing what He did for us by dying on the cross. It is by knowing His love for us. But all this must be made personal to each person. God makes this available to all of us on a one by one basis. If one does not know this truth and experience this forgiveness and relationship available to them, then trials are much harder to understand and to come through appropriately. With faith, hope, and love, each of us who believes is able to walk victoriously through our trials. Only by coming to a knowledge and acceptance of Jesus, will we be able to grow and become more like Him and experience our lives through His eyes.

I never ask God to simply help me get through my trials anymore. Instead, I pray that He helps me have peace during my trials and that He grants me the ability to draw out the full purpose of the trial. It is that type of prayer that has allowed God to be all that He is through me.

Growing up all the way through high school, I never once read a book. I never once wrote a paper. In my junior year in high school, I had to write a term paper. I wrote one, but it was so horrible that my mother had to write a replacement for me so that I would pass my junior year

As a college freshmen, I was required to take English 101. One assignment was to write a five-page paper. I wrote one and received a failing grade. I continued to write papers throughout my first semester, and, of course, was graded with an F with each attempt. Needless to say, I failed English 101. I retook the course in the spring with the same results. Honestly, I had never read a book, my spelling was terrible, and I realized that I had never really been taught English properly in school.

Upon returning home for the summer, I enrolled in an English course through a local Community College. In desperation, on the first day of class, I approached the professor saying, "I have failed English 101 twice now. I have no idea how to read or write. Will you please help me?" Through much time and effort on both of our parts, I ended up with an A in her class.

Despite my success that semester, reading and writing never became any easier for me. To this day I have probably only read fifteen to twenty books. I still cannot read or spell very well. Writing this book, then, is a great testimony to what I can accomplish when I allow God to work through me. There is no way I am able to write a book, but I know who can.

I pray that God will continue to work in me and change me into a new being filled with characteristics of Himself. I pray that I will always be able to see my trials through God's eyes. My journey has not come to an end. Now that I have been transformed from a lion into a lamb, God will transform me into something else - an eagle maybe who learns to soar through my trails with wisdom and strategy. Who knows after that? The only thing I know is that I will continue to have trials and that I will continue to trust God knowing all the while that He loves me continuously and unconditionally and so perfectly. God truly makes my heart sing!

Epilogue

My hope in writing this book is to encourage others through my hardships, to find joy in their lives. "The joy of the Lord is your strength", Nehemiah 8:10. I also want to let people know that they are not alone. If you are feeling alone, I want to enlighten you that there is an amazing, merciful, loving, caring, and kind God out there. He loves you so much that He sent His only son to die on the cross for your sins in order to be able to have a relationship with you. All you have to do is believe John 3:16, "For God so loved the world that he gave his one and only Son, that whoever believes in him shall not perish but have eternal life." The Bible says in Romans 6:23, " All have sinned and fall short of the glory of God." We have all done, thought or said bad things, which the Bible calls "sin." Therefore, we all at one point in our lives are in need of forgiveness.

Thankfully there is a God who can forgive all of our sins. If you truly believe that Jesus is the son of God, then just say this simple prayer: "Dear Lord Jesus, I know I am a sinner, and I ask for your forgiveness. I believe you died for my sins and rose from the dead. I trust and follow you as my Lord and Savior. Come into my heart. Guide my life and help me to do your will. In Jesus name, Amen.

If you said that prayer and truly believe in Jesus, then you will never be alone again. Your hope and joy will be renewed. May the LORD bless you and keep you; The LORD make His face shine upon you, And be gracious to you; the LORD lift up His countenance upon you, And give you peace," Amen.